HIGH TIDES

Wading Through Depression—
Every Day

By

Candace Andrews

Note to Readers:

The names of some persons portrayed
in this book have been changed.

Cover Design & Book Formatting by R.M. ArceJaeger
Cover Photo: laszio/Shutterstock.com

Published by

Palila

ISBN 978-0-9968191-0-7

In memory of
Curtis Steven Andrews,
my brother

HIGH TIDES

I learned not to fear infinity . . .
The sprawl of the wave,
The on-coming water.

—Theodore Roethke,
The Far Field

1 ~ Introduction

"The Life You Save May Be Your Own"
—Flannery O'Conner,
A Good Man Is Hard to Find

Three Kodachrome photographs of my parents and my brother and me, taken one summer in Santa Cruz when I was six years old, dated 1957 on the back, show an azure sky, a cobalt sea, and large, shiny, black rocks jutting out of the sand, all bathed in a luminous blue light. In one of the snapshots, I see myself, a slender girl with long dark hair pulled back in a ponytail, playing in the sand, smiling for the camera.

I don't remember playing in the sand, nor do I remember anything about that trip save two things—riding on Santa Cruz's famous Giant Dipper roller coaster and a giant wave rolling above my head. The roller coaster ride proved more frightening than fun as did my swimming debut in the ocean.

Before going to Santa Cruz, I had taken swimming lessons in the pool reserved for residents of the small suburban tract homes where my family and I lived, and I loved to swim. So, that day at the beach, I was excited when my dad took me out to where the water was up to his neck, and then let me go so that I could swim back to shore. But at some point while swimming back, I tried to stand, perhaps when the wave was cresting over my head, and, of course, I could not get up. Frightened and out of breath, I imagined I was swimming the wrong way, out to sea rather than in toward the seashore. Looking back, I am sure this experience must have lasted only seconds, although it felt like minutes. I kept on swimming and eventually found myself grounded, belly down in the sand, exhausted. From that day forward, I did not like to swim, nor did I like scary amusement park rides.

When I was seven years old, shortly after my first Holy Communion, Mrs. VanAlystine, my best friend's mother and a devout Catholic, gave me a good-deeds bracelet made of string and small rosary-like wooden beads, and every time I made a sacrifice, big or small, I would pull one bead over a small knot in the bracelet. I don't remember how many sacrifices I made or what happened to the bracelet. But this gift is emblematic of what I came to value and what I came to value less—my not being able to bear people who push to the front of the line; those whose voices shout above the rest; those who would, so to speak, always grab for the biggest piece of cake.

When I was ten years old, I went to St. Rose's Church in Sacramento with my grandmother where, before the Mass, we lit candles for people whom we loved, both living and dead.

While lighting a candle, I arched my left hand over the flame, and the fire blistered the inside of my hand from my index finger to the base of my thumb. I hid this injury from my grandmother and everyone, and my hand finally healed on its own. This kind of thing happened to me more than once as a child, where I got hurt and hid my suffering from others. I ponder this now because my experience has led me to believe that whether our suffering is physical or psychological, it is imperative that we seek help.

When I was twelve years old, I went to visit my brother at Stockton State Hospital, again with my beloved grandmother. (Stockton State Hospital was California's first psychiatric hospital, opening in 1851 and closing in 1995.) If my brother, Curtis, had been granted outside privileges, we would have sat underneath a giant magnolia tree on the expansive lawn of the hospital grounds and enjoyed a picnic with bologna sandwiches, potato chips, and Pepsis as we had many times in the past. But this Saturday we had to stay inside in the visitors' room. Although my brother was only fifteen, he was in a men's ward, and when he was in the high of his manic-depressive illness, he was a chain-smoker. Inside the ward, we visited with him in a small room with couches and stand-up ashtrays filled with sand. While my brother smoked and talked—a lot—a young man, his arms covered with snowy cotton gauze from his hands up to his elbows, came in and sat next to me, rocking back and forth. I remember my grandmother holding her purse tightly on her lap, but at twelve years of age I felt special that this young man would want to sit next to me. My brother later told me that this man had tried to set himself afire.

My most detailed memories are from the time I was about twelve years old and later, although looking at photos from earlier periods in my life brings other recollections to mind. A psychiatrist once told me that he could remember anything that happened to him from the time he was a young child if someone only gave him the month and the year, implying that I "must have" forgotten much of my childhood because of some traumatic events that "must have" happened to me early on. But I believe he was wrong. Many, if not most, of us remember those occasions, especially good or especially bad, and we forget much of our day-to-day lives in-between.

I do not remember being depressed as a child. But, as some of the following chapters will show, certain life events may have triggered the major depression that I was already genetically predisposed to have. Much of me as a child foreshadows the adult I would become, better said by William Wordsworth in his line, "The Child is father of the Man [Woman]."[1] At various times in my life, I have remained quiet when I should have spoken out, sacrificing too much of myself, although I generally believe it is better to think of others first. Self-discipline is something I value, and I believe this quality helps me push through my day-to-day depression. I have a secretive nature. And I have, from an early age, had an acute awareness of the suffering of others. Depression interests me not only because I have experienced it for most of my adult life but also because I know others experience it as well. One thing I know for sure is that I am not alone in my suffering.

One in five Americans will experience a depressive episode during his or her lifetime, and that is a staggering statistic. The great writer William Styron who wrote about his major depressive episode in his memoir *Darkness Visible: A Memoir of Madness*—a depressive episode that almost ended his life—went on to experience other major depressive episodes before his death. Unfortunately, experiencing more than one major depressive episode is as common as not.

I have suffered from depression my entire adult life, for about forty years, but I did not have a name for what was troubling me until I was in my late twenties or early thirties (I can't remember exactly). Over the years, I have tried many different classes of antidepressants, some atypical, and many different kinds within those classes. All gave me side effects, but none gave me but minor relief. When I was forty-seven, I had a manic episode and was encouraged by my doctor to try lithium. Lithium has alleviated my daily depression by about 50 percent, which is, to me, the difference between feeling like I'm living and feeling like I'm dying. I still take that medication today.

One doctor says that I live every day with dysthymia (chronic low-grade depression); another says I have "treatment-resistant depression"; but both agree I certainly have Bipolar I (formerly called manic-depression), according to the guidelines in the fifth edition of the *Diagnostic and Statistical Manual of Mental Disorders (DSM-5)*. For me, major depression is the most outstanding and debilitating quality of my bipolar disorder. According to the *DSM-5*, a major depressive episode is characterized by the presence of five or more of the following symptoms during the same two-week period:

❖ Depressed mood most of the day, nearly every day, as indicated by either subjective report (e.g., feels sad, empty, or hopeless) or observation made by others (e.g., appears tearful).

❖ Markedly diminished interest or pleasure in all, or almost all, activities most of the day, nearly every day (as indicated by either subjective account or observation).

❖ Significant weight loss when not dieting or weight gain (e.g., a change of more than 5% body weight in a month), or decrease or increase in appetite nearly every day.

❖ Insomnia or hypersomnia nearly every day.

❖ Psychomotor agitation or retardation nearly every day (observable by others; not merely subjective feelings or restlessness or being slowed down).

❖ Fatigue or loss of energy nearly every day.

❖ Feelings of worthlessness or excessive or inappropriate guilt (which may be delusional) nearly every day (not merely self-reproach or guilt about being sick).

❖ Diminished ability to think or concentrate, or indecisiveness, nearly every day (either by subjective account or as observed by others).

❖ Recurrent thoughts of death (not just fear of dying), recurrent suicidal ideation without a specific plan, or a suicide attempt or a specific plan for committing suicide.[2]

Reprinted with permission from the **Diagnostic and Statistical Manual of Mental Disorders, Fifth Edition** *(Copyright ©2013). American Psychiatric Association.*

In my lifetime, I have experienced at least thirty major depressive episodes characterized by most of the symptoms listed in the *DSM-5* chart for a major depressive episode. There are other criteria for the manic phase of Bipolar I, which I go into at length in Chapter 6. Although I have only had one episode of mania, this episode labeled me as bipolar because one episode of mania or hypomania is a requisite for a bipolar diagnosis. Today I feel fortunate to have received this diagnosis because lithium, a mood stabilizer, is not, at this writing, approved by the Food and Drug Administration (FDA) for use in the treatment of depression outside of the bipolar spectrum.

I have never been hospitalized for my depression, nor have I had electroconvulsive therapy (ECT), although one psychiatrist recommended that treatment for me—more than once—when nothing else seemed to work. Curtis was diagnosed with Bipolar I, but he had a particularly virulent form of this disorder. He experienced continuous and alternating manic and depressive attacks from the time he was fourteen until his early twenties when he was stabilized on lithium.

My brother was committed to Stockton State Hospital in the 1960s, back when people were legally committed to state mental hospitals in California for mental disorders. My brother underwent ECT, without success. (To be fair, the literature says that ECT has changed greatly over the years, but I won't go into that here.) My brother, now deceased, was disabled his whole life from his bipolar disorder even though he was eventually prescribed medications that helped to stabilize his moods. Unfortunately, my brother got sick when he was only a teenager, and his early onset of Bipolar I ravaged his life in many ways.

Fortunately, I have held jobs my whole adult life. I worked for the state of California for seven years; I worked part time while going back to school, at age twenty-eight. Then, after getting my degree, I worked as a high school English teacher for four years before being hired as an English professor at a community college. I worked in my last job as a teacher for twenty-four years before retiring, last year, at the age of sixty-three; however, I still teach one online class. Although I've taken many sick days due to depression throughout the years, and I cancelled one summer school session because of it, I have had the good fortune to have had a productive and meaningful career.

Work, especially teaching, because I have enjoyed it so much, and still enjoy it, has helped give my life stability and purpose. Now, because I am mostly retired, I have the freedom to pursue a different kind of work—writing. I am in the process of learning how to restructure my life for work that requires no time restraints or set routines.

In regard to my personal life, I was married once and have children and grandchildren. I have been in several long-term relationships, but I have been living alone now for about fifteen years.

Both major depression and bipolar disorders have genetic underpinnings. Dr. Kay Redfield Jamison, a professor of psychiatry at the John Hopkins University School of Medicine, who has written many books on bipolar illness, including sharing her own battle with it in her book *An Unquiet Mind*, writes that bipolar disorder "is indisputably genetic"[3]—it runs in families. *Touched with Fire: Manic-Depressive Illness and the Artistic Temperament*, another of Jamison's books, outlines the genealogy of several creative artists and shows a recurring family pattern for this illness. My son is diagnosed with bipolar disorder, and I have a great aunt who spent several years in a mental institution back in the nineteenth century. I am sure my mother suffered from undiagnosed and untreated depression, and I have several other relatives who suffer from depression as well, including one of my grandsons.

Aside from genetics, environmental factors, either positive or negative, can serve as destabilizing triggers for both depression and mania. For myself, when I had my one manic episode, I was under considerable stress. I was leaving a long-term relationship, my therapist was out of town, and I was not sleeping well at all.

Although I consider myself a very private person, I have decided to share my experiences with depression (and my one experience with mania) in the hope that my story may help someone. Managing depression is the focus of this book. I write this book for all those who find themselves depressed for a week, for a month, for six months, or even more, to let you know that someone understands how you are feeling and that you are not alone in your suffering.

I write it particularly for those, like me, who live with depression—every day. I know that we all experience this disorder differently and that we all have a wide variety of coping mechanisms. Some may choose to take medication or to receive ECT; some may choose not to take medication; some may choose to see a therapist, whereas some may not; and some, unfortunately, but perhaps understandably, may choose to self-medicate with illegal drugs or alcohol. I do not judge individuals for what they may do to make themselves feel better, although I do believe there are better and worse choices.

In this book, I want to share with you how I experience depression, what I do to help myself feel better, how I have failed and how I have succeeded, and how I have learned to live with it—sometimes, some days, almost—even happily.

2 ~ What Does Depression Feel Like?

If you can't fly, then run;
if you can't run, walk;
if you can't walk, crawl;
but by all means keep moving.
—Martin Luther King,
Address at Spelman College, April 10, 1960

A t a depression support group I went to only one time,
I met a woman who got up from her bed for only two
hours a day when she was depressed, but I've known others
suffering from depression who are able to go about their daily
routines no matter how terrible they feel. Although I've been in
both places, most of the time I fall somewhere in-between
these two extremes.

First of all, depression is not the same as sadness or grief,
although these can certainly cause great suffering. For any kind
of loss, including bereavement, we grieve for a time; then we

move on. Extended grieving could signal a depressive episode, but sadness and grief over losses of all kinds are certainly normal responses. I know that if I can cry when I'm feeling sad, I am not in too much trouble, because when depression overtakes me, my emotions, aside from fear, anxiety, and anguish, get tangled in a knot deep inside of me, inaccessible. When deeply depressed, I am scattered, slow, confused, stupid. My waking and nighttime dreams seem to vanish; words, usually my strength, fail me.

I sometimes think of depression as a *Great Blankness*, although, to use an oxymoron, I feel nothing and I feel horrible, both at the same time. When I am deeply depressed, I cannot organize anything. I cannot alphabetize a set of papers or sort the dirty dishes in my kitchen so that I can wash them. My body feels like lead; my mind a giant fuzz ball. Fortunately, I've learned not to beat myself up by these annoyances but to simply set aside the things I absolutely cannot seem to do, no matter how small, until I feel better.

When I am significantly depressed, I feel as if I am in a huge concrete labyrinth with no view overhead. Once inside, a giant door locks after me, and as I crawl, walk, and/or run trying to find my way out, I grow more fearful. It is cold, the walls are barely as wide as I am, and there is nothing, and *especially no one*, to grab a hold of. As I navigate through the labyrinth, I come to many different passageways—all dead-ends. I imagine the labyrinth glaring white; never is there a spot of color; all is empty, barren, desolate. The harder I try to find my way out of this hard and unforgiving landscape, the more lost and fearful I become. I am like a child, trying to maneuver through something that seems beyond my understanding and skill.

Sometimes it feels as if someone or something is chasing

me, and this speeds up my movement, as well as my anxiety, and leads me farther and farther into the circuitous and coiling route. When I feel I am making some headway, the labyrinth shifts its orientation, so what was forward is now backward or what was backward is now sideways. This is especially disconcerting because spatial navigation is not my strong point. I become consumed with what Styron calls a "fidgety restlessness,"[4] which, I know, is counterproductive to the task at hand. However, I try repeatedly to stop and clear my mind before moving forward, to get a grip on myself. For one thing I've learned is that the more I let my anxiety overtake me, the harder this thing will chase me. But, fast or slow, I know that movement is imperative. To stop moving, to give up, means that a worse fate surely awaits me.

Perhaps a better and more precise way to explain how my depression feels has to do with *water*. Water is both a powerful and universal symbol for the unconscious, and although water is also the source of life, regeneration, and purification, I would rather look at water than be immersed in it. Ever since that summer day in Santa Cruz, I have had dreams where I was drowning.

My feelings surrounding water are paradoxical. Like everyone, I find such things as springs, streams, rivers, lakes, and of course, the ocean, not only beautiful, but comforting and spiritual as well. The sound of water is hypnotic and relaxing. I enjoy walking into water up to my ankles or sometimes even up to my knees, as long as I can walk right back out again. But I don't like to swim, although I *can* swim. I hate that water is cold; I hate that water can be treacherous. And, I hate the feeling that being in high water brings, like my legs and arms are heavy.

When I go to see my internist, the nurse always asks me if I am in pain (referring, of course, to physical pain). If I answer "Yes," the nurse says, "On a scale of one to ten, what's your pain level?" This always puzzles me because there is no context for a one or a ten. So, I always imagine that ten is the pain of childbirth, the most excruciating physical pain I have ever experienced. This makes it easier for me to give a number.

Because I have developed the habit of monitoring my day-to-day depression, I also use a one-to-ten scale when I think about how I'm feeling on any given day. The context I use is that of a water table for, again, water is hard to move about in (unless one is swimming or floating). This is the context for my numbering system:

Depression Level 1: The water is up to my ankles. I am slower, but I can still move about easily. At levels 1 through 4, I can pretty much "pretend" that I am not depressed, certainly in public and when I am around others. I may overcompensate by acting more extroverted and friendly than I actually feel. In the early stages of depression, time feels as if it is elongated. Simple tasks like showering and dressing seem to take longer than usual. At the same time, my focus on small things, such as buttoning a button, is magnified.

Depression Level 5: The water is up to my waist. I am much slower, and I must push ahead in order to work and do my daily tasks. My mind is foggy at times. The labyrinth example mentioned previously characterizes how I am feeling at level 5. Depression level 5 often signals the beginning of a major depressive episode. However, my depression level sometimes stops at a 5 and goes back down.

Depression Level 10: The water is over my head; I am drowning.

I would say I am usually between levels 2 and 4 on my depression water table scale. Since I have been taking lithium, for about sixteen years now, my depression has gone over level 5 about twelve times. (But lithium has **significantly** diminished my depression from day to day.) Over level 5, I am in trouble. As my depression worsens, I begin feeling scattered and eventually more and more unable to move or to help myself. (See *Chapter 8: Deep Water* for more about this.)

A friend asked me if I am able to tell whether I am headed for a major depressive episode, and all I can say is, "Not most of the time." I experience no quantifiable sign such as the aura that some migraine sufferers experience. Negative environmental factors may be present or not. When I monitor my depression, I am content if the water is standing still, at a low level. However, it can rise so slowly as to be imperceptible or rush suddenly upward. I have experienced feeling pretty well one day, and the very next day I have had to call in sick to work (when I was working full time) or cancel my appointments. Significant slowing down mentally, including difficulty in organizing anything, is often the first clue that I am headed for, or already in, deep water.

Personally and somewhat atypically, my depression is generally worse in spring and summer, when the weather is warmer, and better in the fall and winter, when the weather is cooler, although I can find neither rhyme nor reason for this. However, I often manage to help keep my depression in an acceptable range by caring for myself through various activities. (See *Chapter 5: Strategies for Escape.*)

If you have ever cared for plants, or pets, or any living thing, you notice that if not well cared for they sometimes simply exist or barely survive. And while merely surviving is sometimes the very best I can do, and maybe the very best you can do, the goal is for me—for us—to grow, to prosper, to thrive.

3 ~ Sweet, Sweeter, Sweetest (Food)

One cannot think well, love well,
sleep well, if one has not dined well.
—Virginia Woolf,
A Room of One's Own

F ried chicken, rocky road ice cream, sea salt and vinegar potato chips, Ruben sandwiches, any kind of cake, but especially chocolate cake with chocolate frosting or cheesecake—these are some of my favorite comfort foods. My relationship with food is a part of my life affected by my depression. Depressed people are likely to overeat or undereat, and although I have done both, I am more likely to undereat or not eat at all. When very depressed, food—flavorful, hearty, wonderful food—falls to the bottom of my "to-do" list. However, I do understand how feeling full can be comforting and relaxing; I do understand how eating more than we should can

18

both bring a sense of well-being and make us feel guilty at the same time. Almost no one wants to gain weight, and no one wants to feel even worse just by eating.

Overeating, soon, and always, makes me feel worse. I enjoy those extreme weight-loss shows like *The Biggest Loser* because they demonstrate how with loads of willpower and good support, many can overcome a lifetime of not getting enough exercise and bad eating choices. But add to that a depressive component, and the odds of beating the food cravings surely become ten times more difficult.

When I am very, very depressed, food nauseates me, especially the smell of food. I know enough about eating to know that when I do not eat (I've gone as long as three days eating nothing, only drinking water), my body metabolizes muscle rather than fat. When I finally just force myself to eat, which I always will do, I'll eat a few spoonfuls of cereal, a few bites of an apple or some orange slices, or a piece of toast, eating small portions of food at various times throughout the day. If I cannot stomach food, I will at least drink some milk or juice. Once I begin eating, my aversion to food eventually dissipates. Of course, not eating always makes me lose weight, temporarily, but it's not muscle that I want to lose. My whole adult life, in spite of my eating habits, I've remained close to the same weight, which is around 130 to 135 pounds. I am around five feet four inches tall, so my weight is pretty average.

When my depression goes above a 5, I do not leave the house much. Because I like simple foods and am a frugal eater, I usually have enough food in the house to last me until my depression passes. I always have eggs, bread, butter, milk, pasta, spaghetti sauce, and the usual staples we all keep in our pantries. I usually have fruit juice and fruits and vegetables. I always have rice and beans and some canned foods. I always also have ramen. Ramen, with broccoli, carrots, and slices of hard-boiled eggs, is not such a bad choice. I always have some frozen food, including some frozen meat. I have been told that I have nothing to eat in my house. But, for me, without a family in the house or anyone to cook for other than myself, my pantry is usually sufficient to get me through a rough patch.

My depression is around a 4 today. According to my water table system, the water is not yet up to my waist, but it is over my knees and climbing. I am feeling slow. Not only is my body slower, but also when I speak, I notice that my voice has a somewhat hollow sound, and sometimes it is just hard to get my words out. Although I don't want to be around people, I have nothing in the house that I feel like eating, so I go grocery shopping.

I buy some kale for my juicer, a block of extra-sharp cheddar cheese, a quart of organic apple juice, some grass-fed sirloin steak, and two cantaloupes (on sale). I also buy eight Danish butter pastries, three of which I eat in the car on my drive home, knowing full well that I crave sweets when I am depressed, knowing full well that their soporific and feel-good effects will wear off in a few hours, leaving me feeling worse rather than better. At home I have all kinds of fruit—grapes, oranges, apples—any of which would be a much better choice than the pastries, but when I pass these sweets in the grocery aisle, I cannot resist them because (a) I love pastries and (b) I know that pure sugar will make me feel better temporarily, and I want to feel better. I give about a second's thought to not buying them.

When I'm depressed, I usually undereat. Unfortunately, even when I undereat, I will often still grab for that donut, cookie, or piece of cake because any of these will make me feel better, if just for a minute. After I get home, I eat two more pastries then push the other three to the bottom of the garbage so that I will not be tempted to fish them out later.

I know that to feel best, I need to maintain stable blood sugar throughout the day by eating healthful and nutritious meals. But today, I will be gentle with myself about my failings, and so I have two choices. I can (1) choose to feel bad that I've eaten five pastries in an hour or so, or (2) choose to feel good that I threw three away. Today I go with the latter.

I was raised in a working-class family, and growing up, a typical dinner consisted of some kind of meat, some kind of potato, and some kind of vegetable. We ate all kinds of vegetables. Sometimes we had tomatoes (with mayonnaise), broccoli (with mayonnaise), asparagus (with mayonnaise), cauliflower (with mayonnaise), or artichokes (with mayonnaise). I know many people would rather shoot themselves than add anything to their vegetables, and I suppose eating virgin vegetables is better. But eating, for me, particularly when I am feeling well, has a lot to do with pleasure. So, I still eat many of my vegetables with mayonnaise.

Because I live alone, no one, unfortunately, is going to cook or prepare meals for me; on the other hand, I am fortunate that I am not expected to cook or prepare meals for anyone else. In the middle of a depressive episode, I have learned to make relatively simple meals with little or no cooking. I use a juicer (or just drink juice, or milk); I make sandwiches; I eat hot or cold cereal; I eat fresh fruits and vegetables; sometimes, I resort to frozen foods.

Tonight for dinner, I eat smoked salmon (the kind found already cooked in the meat section of a grocery store), a piece of toast with butter, half an avocado (with mayonnaise), two tangerines, and two glasses of milk. I know that when I am depressed, I will crave something sweet but that it is sweeter to have a piece of fruit than candy, cake, or Danish pastries, and that the sweetest thing I can do for myself is to eat healthful foods.

For tomorrow, I make a short list of things I will **not do.** I will not, for tomorrow, at least:

❖ Put junk food into my body

❖ Watch TV all day long

❖ Smoke

❖ Stay in inside all day

❖ Wallow in my misery

Concerning food, we all know what is good, better, and best to eat. Try to eat healthily, but if you fail, don't beat yourself up too much. Feeling ashamed or guilty is counterproductive. Focus on taking care of yourself in small ways. I enjoy drinking coffee, so I may treat myself to a latte. I enjoy sandwiches, so I may buy my favorite kind of bread. Taking care of yourself in small ways does not only concern eating. I enjoy baths, so I may take a bubble bath; I enjoy music, so I may download some of my favorite songs. Whatever brings you small pleasures, and is not bad for you, do!

4 ~ Support: Who Will Listen?

> You never really understand a person until
> you consider things from his point of
> view—until you climb inside of his skin
> and walk around in it.
>
> —Harper Lee,
> *To Kill a Mockingbird*

I went to a depression support group once. (I have been willing to try many things, at least once, to see if they may help me feel better.) The support group was, if I remember correctly, affiliated with a hospital. I had imagined that it would be held in a small space with a small group of people who had issues with depression, and maybe a leader, but it was held in an auditorium. All I remember is that there was a stage and that someone with a microphone talked about depression in general for a bit; then other people came up and talked more personally about how they experienced depression. I listened and heard from the woman who only got up for two hours a day when she was depressed. And, I learned that not only did she get up for only two hours a day, but, as she told her audience, she got up for only two hours a day for weeks at a time. After listening to her, I thought that maybe she should have been in the hospital. But the group thing was just not for me.

I am an introvert, and, like most introverts, I do not like to share a lot with other people. I have a small circle of friends. They know I have issues with depression, but I never talk about this with any of them at length. I have gotten very good at pretending I'm not depressed, at developing a persona. Kurt Vonnegut said, "We are what we pretend to be."[5] True or not, pretending has allowed me to teach my classes and to carry on with my life with some degree of normality. I am not the type of person who wants to be "bleeding" all over her friends and family when I'm depressed, so I try my best to keep my difficult moods to myself. And, although a support group or group therapy or talking to a close friend or family member may work for many, these avenues are not for me.

One thing that has helped me cope with depression is talk therapy (with a professional therapist, a psychologist). I know that therapy is expensive—very expensive. I have been fortunate that my medical insurance will pay about three-fourths of each of twelve visits per year. I have had enough money to pay the remainder and to pay out of pocket for more. I know that I am very lucky to have had the money to do this. I recently told a friend of mine I had clocked in thousands of hours over my lifetime with a therapist. His reply, "So much money!" My reply to him, "For me, it's been worth it!"

I have seen several psychiatrists (both men and women) briefly over the years because only medical doctors (not psychologists) can prescribe medication. However, I did see one psychiatrist monthly for more than a year, a woman. She was overly rational, too directive, and somewhat cold. It took me quite a while to come to this conclusion and to terminate therapy with her because my feelers are a little off when I'm depressed, and I sometimes don't trust my own instincts.

I have also seen four psychologists over the course of my lifetime, three men and one woman. I saw one at the college medical center, on and off, for a year when I went back to college in my thirties. His advice was almost free because I got a student discount. He did talk therapy as well as body work. Once he asked me to scream, yelling out all of my frustrations into the universe, and that was something I was neither comfortable with nor willing to do. I saw another therapist for three or four sessions (he was just too probing and bossy) and another for about three months (she and I just didn't click).

What I know for sure is that shopping around for a therapist is important although it may seem intimidating, if not impossible, to do when you are very depressed. Needless to say, consider your own personality, your values, and what you need from therapy, including the kind of therapist whom you will be comfortable with. Personally, I don't like the directive approach, with someone telling me what I should or should not do, but some people like that method. I cannot tolerate a therapist who is judgmental and patronizing, wants to continually delve into my childhood for root causes, or thinks he or she knows more than me about everything. Of course therapists have degrees and specialized training, but they have not lived your life.

Unfortunately, it took me many years to find the right therapist, and I ultimately did so by trial and error. At first, it is hard to know what a therapist will be like, or even if you will like him or her, which I find very important. I was willing to try out several therapists until I found the right one. Today, I believe that if I had followed my instincts more than my intellect, I may have found the right one sooner. Ultimately, he or she just has to be the right one for you. It is your life that's at stake. Finding a good therapist is not the same as trying to find a doctor for a stomachache.

My last and current psychologist/therapist, I'll call him David, I have seen, overall, for about seventeen years. (My internist now prescribes my medication.) I started seeing this therapist about twenty years ago, although I've taken a one-year hiatus and a two-year hiatus during that time. At times I have seen him once a week, at times once a month, and sometimes more frequently or infrequently, but, perhaps more important, I knew he was *there*, if I ever needed to talk. At a particularly difficult time in my life, David came to the office on a Sunday to see me because I was in crisis. I greatly appreciated that, and he didn't charge me extra because it was a weekend.

I know that most insurance companies, and even some therapists, think it best if you get in and out with as few sessions as possible—diagnose the problem, talk about the solution, and fix it. But my ultimate goal was getting through the rest of my life with some quality of life, gaining some understanding of what led me to the place I was in, and learning how to manage my depression. Therapy is the one great gift I have given myself. And, although I know many will not understand the length of time (or the amount of money) I have spent there, I don't regret one second of it.

The first time I saw David, he immediately asked me to call him by his first name. I was in my forties, so I felt comfortable with that. He was soft-spoken, like I am; he was pleasant; he was very humble compared to the other mental health professionals I had dealt with; he was very intelligent with a background in both comparative literature (that was a plus) and Jungian psychology. And he did not ask me too many questions. Rather, he just let me talk, and he mostly just listened. (David has always encouraged me to talk about anything that is on my mind—my childhood, my depression, my dreams, my children, my relationships.) Anyhow, I had had a dream I wanted to talk about, and although I don't remember exactly what he said about it now, over the years David has helped me analyze my own dreams, so that I have become my own dream expert.

I believe in dreams; I believe dreams are messages from the unconscious; I believe that if we pay attention to what our dreams are telling us, we can understand ourselves better and even grow and change. The dream I brought with me that day goes as follows:

> I am on a ship, and a lion is chasing me. I am scared to death of him. We are in the interior of the ship, and no matter how fast I run, the lion is right behind me. Finally, the ship docks, and I step into a small cabin where there is an old wise man. I tell him about the lion, and he reaches up and opens a cupboard over his head and takes out a couple of huge baby bottles, full of milk. Then, he turns to me and says, "Feed the lion."

Having been a literature major in college, I already knew something about symbols, so I knew that a lion is a strong, powerful symbol for the masculine, a solar symbol. Real lions *can* be dangerous, and in this dream I was very afraid. I was on a ship, which seemed to be going nowhere; I was in an interior space, so I knew this dream was telling me something about my inward state of being. Now milk bottles, full of milk no less, are certainly symbols for the feminine, lunar symbols. The wise man seemed to be telling me that by feeding the "masculine" side of myself I could integrate the feminine into the masculine and tame the lion.

This dream spoke to me because, at the time, I was in a relationship where I was not standing up for myself, and both the relationship and I were going nowhere. I was allowing myself to be beaten down because I was keeping all of my feelings in; I was just too passive. In effect, I was running from, rather than facing, the more masculine side of my nature. By infusing the feminine (represented by the milk bottles) into the masculine, I would be able to regain my own personal power and stand up for myself.

David talked to me that day about how symbols in dreams are both personal and universal, and how the lion is a great universal symbol, an archetype. He also told me that, usually, every character in the dream—man, woman, or beast—represents different sides of oneself. So, the wise man was *me* too. If I saw the wise man as a part of me, I already knew, like he did, what I needed to do. Before I left that day, David duplicated a page from a book by the South African-born writer Laurens van der Post, a page about lions, and he highlighted some passages for me. That small action struck me as quite extraordinary.

It took me a few more years to leave the bad relationship I was in. I frequently talked with David about this; he didn't push me; he said I would leave "when I was ready." And one day, that's exactly what happened. My significant other had come into the house, setting some grocery bags on the table after having been shopping, and out of nowhere, I started sobbing. I told him I needed to leave the relationship, that I just couldn't do it anymore, that it was making me sick. However, within a week, I experienced a manic episode, perhaps partly precipitated by my decision. But, I knew I had to leave. And, if I hadn't been talking with David about this relationship, I am not sure that I ever would have left.

Ten years later, I had another simple, but powerful dream, which painfully reminded me that I had not yet learned my lesson. The dream goes as follows:

> I go to visit a sadu, an Indian holy man. I say to him, "How can I relieve my suffering?" He answers by placing a crystal necklace full of menstrual blood around my neck.

During this time in my life, I was in another destructive relationship. The man I was with was extremely intelligent and equally egotistical and manipulative. I was suffering in this relationship, but I was mesmerized by his intellect and our mutual sexual attraction. The wise sadu's message is to encircle myself (the necklace) with the power of the feminine. And although, culturally, we may think of the feminine as weak or passive, the opposite is true. In the dream, the feminine that I need to encircle myself with in order to relieve my suffering is wise, strong, transparent (like the crystal), and equipped with hidden powers. (Crystals are symbols of divination and wisdom.)

The sadu gives me a talisman, the necklace full of menstrual blood, to protect me from the "evil" influence this man had over me. Blood is a solar symbol, and, of course, the very stuff of life itself. However, **menstrual blood** belongs to women alone; in some cultures, menstruating women are thought to be sacred and powerful; in others, they are thought to be unclean. Regardless, many men are just not too fond of a menstruating partner; certainly many men will not have intercourse with a woman who is menstruating.

As in the lion dream, my psyche was telling me to own my own powers, to stand up for myself. Finally, I did leave this relationship as well. Not right after the dream, but eventually. Of course, I can understand this all more clearly now. Hindsight *is* twenty-twenty.

Personal growth can be a slow and painful process. Some of us, like myself, make the same mistakes over and over again, despite the help of an effective therapist. One thing I have learned about dreams from David is that we will have the same dream, presented in different ways, until we finally "get it."

Looking at my dreams was one part of my therapeutic process. In a typical session with David, we would talk about a particular interesting dream or about something in my life that was troubling me. I would leave most sessions in a thoughtful mood, and I would think about what we had talked about many times during the week and before our next meeting. Sometimes I left hopeful, sometimes even happy. And once in a while, I would leave angry.

Before one of these angry departures, I had been talking about my depression, and David said to me, "Many people would be jealous of what you have." What he meant by this was that many people would be happy to have a good job, family and friends who cared about them, and enough money not to have to worry too much. To be fair, words can be misconstrued and often are. But, this statement made me more than furious because I felt David was denigrating my feelings, and I was feeling badly.

The late comedian Robin Williams, who committed suicide in 2014 (he was born in the same year as I was, and I *loved* Robin Williams!), ostensibly had everything. He was married to a younger and beautiful woman; he was brilliant, talented, and famous; he had children who were healthy; he seemingly had more than enough money. Perhaps it was his diagnosis of Parkinson's that led him to suicide. We will never know. But the face he showed to the world and his interior state did not match. Depression is not about externals; any depressed person can have a good job or not, money or not, friends and family or not. Depression is about an interior state, and much of the time, others do not understand what *a hell of a place* that interior state can be.

David and I later talked about his words that so angered me, and he apologized. I still remember those, but I also remember something else he said that same day he said those inflammatory words. He said, "Just look outside." It was springtime, and through the sliding glass door in his office, I could see a tree with bright green new leaves, a bush festooned with tiny white flowers, and water trickling into a small pond, all bathed in sunlight. Without having to say it, David was both referring to the beauty and mystery of nature and also reminding me, in his way, to live in the moment. Being *here*, now, in the present, is one of the most important lessons I've learned from therapy.

My relationship with my therapist is complex. It is more

than an affiliation, yet is it is both more, and less, than a close friendship. When I feel frustrated and sometimes overwhelmed because of the many different kinds of feelings that arise in me, both during and after our sessions (both positive and negative), David says, "There is no transference without counter-transference." By this he means that feelings arise in both of us because of our work together; therapy is not a one-sided proposition. He is saying that he is part of the process as much as I am, that the interplay of conscious and unconscious forces in therapy affects us both.

Transference, put simply, is the displacement of feelings, often originating in the unconscious, onto a surrogate. Transference is a part of most relationships to some degree, although it is often more intense in the therapeutic one. Transference, including projection, is an extremely complex subject, but it is something that must be addressed in long-term therapy.

Therapy, for me, has been an opportunity to have a healing and soulful connection with another human being in a relationship like no other. All the kinds of feelings, both positive and negative, that arise in any close relationship arise during the course of therapy. David and I have argued with one another, we have laughed together, and I, at least, have cried—many times. And even though there were a few times when I have felt frustrated with David, I know for sure there were times when he felt frustrated with me. David knows many things about me that no one else does, and I know, absolutely, that my secrets are safe with him.

Even as I write this, my relationship with David is undergoing a drastic change. For medical reasons, he closed his practice and moved out of state. He referred most of his clients to another therapist, although he will keep in touch with a few over the phone; a few more he will see monthly or less often when he comes down to Sacramento for his own medical appointments. Right now, I fall into the latter category, but, realistically, I know there will come a time when we will have to terminate our work, and I will just have to move on without his support.

How will I do this? I suppose I will know for sure when that time comes. However, I know that at this stage in my life I will not seek another therapist. Everything I have learned from our work together lives inside of me and will continue to influence me until the day I die. I can best describe my relationship with David as a gift. Certainly, whatever the future may hold, and as I told my friend earlier, "For me, it's been worth it!"

Every person who suffers from depression needs someone with whom he or she can honestly talk and relate; it may or may not be a member or members of a support group, a friend, a family member, a significant other, a spouse, or a therapist. Every person who suffers from depression **deserves** this. All people suffering from depression need their feelings validated to know that they are **not** narcissistic or crazy.

Depressed people need someone who is kind, understanding, and nonjudgmental who will listen attentively, a person who knows that depressives cannot just snap out of it, any more than they can change their eye color. Depressed individuals need someone **to bear witness to their suffering**. Having someone confirm that their suffering is real will enable them to find the inner strength to discover their own solutions and to create, for themselves, healthful and meaningful lives.

5 ~ Strategies for Escape

Tell me, what is it you plan to do
with your one wild and precious life?

—Mary Oliver,
New and Selected Poems

I n the novel *The Secret Life of Bees* by Sue Monk Kidd, Lily, the young protagonist, catches some bees in a jar and puts the lid on. Days later, Lily unscrews the lid of the jar, but the bees, thinking they still trapped, "crawled on their stalk legs around the curved perimeters of the glass as if the world had shrunk to that jar."[6] Learned helplessness, a term first coined by psychologist Martin Seligman, and exemplified by the example of the bees in the jar, is thought to be one of the underlying causes of depression. David, my therapist, presented the idea of learned helplessness to me very gently. He felt that because I had been depressed for so long, and because I had suffered so many major depressive episodes, I had little knowledge of what it felt like to be set free from my "jar"—my depressive moods—and he implied I had given up trying to fight this thing.

When David first presented this idea to me, many years ago now, there surely was some truth in what he said. It did give me something to think about. But, over the years, and especially since I have been taking lithium, which has lessened my depressive symptoms significantly, I have learned various ways to escape from that jar. Some of my strategies will be explored further in this chapter.

Morning brings my first and most difficult daily battle, my cares and worries compressed and pronounced, my anxiety high. If I were predisposed to negative thinking, Billie Holiday's song title "Good Morning, Heartache" could be my mantra. However, to linger too long under the silky sheets and soft blankets is a mistake, for I know I will feel better as soon as I get up and start moving. I have some sleep issues, so when I wake up, I do not feel that well. I can fall asleep rather quickly, but often I will wake up at 3:00 a.m. or 4:00 a.m. after having gone to bed at 11:00, and I won't fall back asleep. I have tried everything, from going to bed earlier; to eating oatmeal or toast; to drinking warm milk; to getting up and reading, taking a bath, or cleaning my house; to, well, just about everything! I have taken over-the-counter sleep aids, and I have a prescription for a sleep medication, which I do take if my insomnia is unrelenting, but usually I just lie in bed and try to clear my mind or meditate. If nothing else works, I just "suck it up."

Like many depressives, I feel worse in the morning and often better as the day progresses. But, for the past ten years or so, unless I am in the middle of a major depressive episode (see *Chapter 8: Deep Water* for more about this), I will just not allow myself to languish in bed after I wake up, for the longer I stay in bed, the worse I begin to feel. The temptation to stay in bed is still present when I'm more mildly depressed, but one thing I have found that helps me avoid this is making lists.

List Making

My basic routine now that I am partially retired (I teach only online, so I don't have to *be* anywhere) is to get out of bed at 7:00 or 8:00 a.m., make myself a cup of coffee, and turn on the news or a morning show—*Good Day Sacramento* is my current favorite—and make a list. I have developed the habit of list making because it helps me set priorities, it helps me focus, and it forces me to get out of the house. When I make a list, I usually complete three-fourths of it by the day's end. Before I made lists, I would just ruminate and ruminate about things I needed to do, and, usually, I would end up not doing much of anything except watching television or reading all day—not that reading is bad.

Sometimes my lists are "not-do" lists, like the little one at the end of Chapter 3. But mostly they are "to-do" lists. Here is one that I made for yesterday, a Thursday, with the items in no particular order:

- ❖ Work on book
- ❖ Exercise with weights
- ❖ Take a walk
- ❖ Finish quizzes for *American Women Writers*
- ❖ Go to Target for cleaning supplies

❖ Begin packing for Saturday's trip

❖ Do some "brain games" on computer

❖ Wash clothes

❖ Water flowers in backyard

❖ Call piano tuner

❖ Finish reading book (*The Queen Must Die: And Other Affairs of Bees and Men* by William Longgood)

This, of course, is not everything I would do in a day, but it gives me a start. When more depressed, I make the list before I've even gotten out of bed, and it would include more obvious things that I nonetheless might fail to do if I did not write them down, things like:

❖ Get out of bed

❖ Make coffee

❖ Turn on *Good Day*

❖ Take a shower and wash my hair . . .

Once, when I was stuck and depressed and felt that nothing whatsoever interested me, I made a list and came up with more than twenty things I might like to do someday. Three of these included:

❖ Make more scrapbooks for my photos

❖ Read about different breeds of dogs, because one day, I **will** get a dog

❖ Explore on the Internet public mines or areas in

California where I can search for things like crystals, sunstones, or arrowheads

Writing lists, a form of brainstorming, seems to tap into some part of me that I would not have had access to if I didn't write it down. And, contrary to my depressed mood that "told" me I was not interested in anything, I found through this exercise that I was, indeed, interested in many things.

Writing

I love to write, whether an e-mail to a friend, a personal letter, an inscription in a card, a poem, a journal entry, a story, or an essay. Of course I love to receive personal written things as well. I do not write in a journal every day or even every month, but I do write in one when I feel the need to sort out my thoughts. This always helps me when I have no one to talk with. In fact, it is different, and sometimes even better, than talking to someone else, for journal writing is talking to oneself, and I don't have to share what I write with anyone!

Not long ago, my daughter and I got into a serious fight. Because I was not speaking to her for a few days, she wrote me a letter. Because I was afraid to open the letter, afraid that she would say things that would hurt my feelings, I did not open her letter for two days. Before I opened it, I wrote a journal entry to myself about all of my fears about the letter. Then I wrote a journal entry composed as a letter to David—a letter I never planned to give him—outlining my fears about the letter. After doing these two things, I had fewer problems opening the letter, which actually proved to be nothing bad at all.

I find journal writing to be best for me when I'm feeling particularly bad. In fact, I wish I had the resolve to write in a journal more often. Reading back through my many journals over the years has been illuminating and interesting, enabling me to remember so many things I had forgotten—both good and bad.

Some therapists as well as medical doctors incorporate things like writing and art (painting and drawing) into their work. I have read that these kinds of expressive therapies are very beneficial to many people. That being said, one therapist gave me "homework" in the form of writing assignments (the first assignment was to write a brief autobiography of myself). And although I generally love to write, I did not like these assignments at all. I did not know him well enough to share what he was asking me to share, at least not all at one time, and I know I omitted things that maybe should have been included.

When I know I am writing for an audience, even an audience of one, the content of my writing changes, sometimes a lot, sometimes just ever so slightly. Diaries for young people sometimes come with a little lock and key, a signal screaming *"Private!"* Of course, private writing can be shared at the writer's discretion. When I have taught writing classes and my students share their writing by distributing copies of it to others and then reading it aloud in small groups, I always tell them that this process changes their writing from private to public. I encourage them to omit anything they don't want anyone else—including me—to hear or read.

Aside from journal writing, I also like to write poetry. Sometimes I share my poetry, and sometimes I simply write it for myself. I write about many things, but once I was trying to personify my depression, and the following poem just came out. I saw my depression as a dark sister who had great power over me. This is what I wrote:

Dark Sister
Midnight Princess

Swaddle me
in purple robes;
rock me
in opium dreams;
hide me
from the napalm glare
of business, banks, and Wall Street afternoons.

Inside your shady garden,
among foxgloves and fairy wands,
where tree ferns grow taller than human beings
and angel tears muddy the fertile ground,
I will sit and wait.

Among sorrows
deeper than God,
I will find my way.

Walk with me.
Talk to me.
Fly me from the marble speak
of scientists, counselors, and kings.

Royal Lady—
Shadow Artist—

Be my friend.
Let me live.

I wrote this poem in my early forties, but analyzing it now, I see this was another case, like the lion dream in Chapter 4, of not integrating my powers, in this case, the power of my stronger, "darker" feminine. Certainly the "dark sister" is *me* as well. Doing some Active Imagination, a process in which one dialogues with dream or other fictional characters, might help me to analyze this poem further. But I didn't want to analyze it too much. I very much liked it when I wrote it twenty years ago, and I like it still. It shows a healthy distrust of consumerism and institutions and men who think that their gender alone gives them power over me.

Active Imagination is a technique developed by Carl G. Jung to help translate and integrate the unconscious into images through visualization or works of art. Contemporary author and Jungian analyst Robert A. Johnson writes about a similar method in his book *Inner Work: Using Dreams and Active Imagination for Personal Growth.* You don't have to be a writer or an artist to use this technique, and you can share your writing with whomever you choose. Whether or not anyone else reads what I write, I still find it helpful to explore my innermost feelings.

I want to share one more poem because it deals with water, and it is a healing view of water. I wrote this about ten years ago.

Antidote for Sorrow

Supplies:
One loaf of bread.
One jar of jam—boysenberry, strawberry, apricot, or peach.

One table knife.
One thermos, full of cold water.

In the morning, find a river.
Wade in it up to your waist.
Feel the cold.
Feel the current swimming
around your legs and middle.
Bend down, carefully.
Scoop up two handfuls of pebbles.

When your legs are good and numb,
walk slowly back to shore.
Sit on a warm rock.
Open your fists.
Lift your palms upwards, toward the sunlight.
Notice how the pebbles change colors as they dry.
Watch the pollen
drift across the river on the breeze.

When your arms hurt so much you can't hold them
up any longer,
blow the pebbles back into the river.
Cross your arms around your waist.
Rock back and forth.

Listen to the river. Listen to the river.
Listen to the river.

Cry.

When you are good and hungry,
take out the loaf of bread.
Spread each piece with jam, your favorite kind.
Eat the whole loaf.
Wash it down with cold water from your thermos.

Sit there until evening, just breathing,
just breathing.

I have participated in writing groups at various times in my life when I have wanted to share my more public writing. There, I share my writing with others, others share their writing with me, and we give each other feedback. Finding people whom you trust and enjoy being around is important for everyone, certainly for people who suffer from depression. However, I must admit, I have not been very good at doing this for myself.

Walking, Running, Hiking

I am not a runner, but I included *running* in the header because running, even more than walking, gets the blood flowing and raises endorphin levels. Very occasionally I sprint, alternating between running a short distance and walking very fast, but most of all I take a walk or hike. I like to walk; in fact, I read somewhere that a ten-minute walk can lift your spirits for two hours.

If my depression is in its normal range for me, between levels 2 and 4, I go for a walk as much as every other day. My three favorite parks near my house in Sacramento are Land Park, Capitol Park, and McKinley Park. I can drive or walk to

Land Park, although usually I drive, and both of the other two parks are a short driving distance from my house. All of the parks have walking trails, and once there, I walk around the path, usually walking about two to four miles, depending on how many times I go around. Occasionally, I walk with a friend, but most often I walk by myself.

When walking alone, I am able to set my own pace; I often like to stop and look at things—the ducks in Land Park, the war memorials in Capitol Park, the rose garden in McKinley Park. Walking *always* makes me feel better. It is one of the best things I can do for myself.

I also like to hike. Unlike with walking, I seldom hike alone. I have a small group of hiking friends, but I usually hike with just one or two others. Sometimes we go over to Point Reyes National Seashore or hike up Mount Diablo. But, my favorite hiking places are those with high granite peaks or waterfalls, or both, in the higher elevations. In California, Mount Shasta, Burney Falls, McCloud Falls, Silver Lake, Carson Pass, and the Markleeville area are some of my favorites. Lake Tahoe is another place with fabulous views and hiking trails. Hiking, even more than walking, gives me a wonderful workout. On a typical day hike, I walk about six miles, sometimes more.

Also, just being in nature, with the stunning scenery, makes me feel better. Hiking with a good friend is a pleasant experience, and I enjoy the company. The beauty of the natural world, whether I'm feeling good or feeling badly, is something that always and inevitably lifts my spirits.

Decorating

A friend once said to me, "You should enjoy being in every room in your house." His words resonated with me because my living space is important to me, and I know it influences how I feel. I rent a small (750-square-foot) one-bedroom duplex, which is perfect for me right now. I don't need large or fancy. I need comfortable, warm, and cheerful.

I moved three years ago, and at that time I decided to simplify my life by getting rid of things I did not really need or want anymore. I gave away some furniture, some linens, some dishes, thirty-five boxes of books I knew I would never look at again, and various odds and ends. I wanted all of the things that surrounded me to be what I truly wanted, needed, or enjoyed. Doing this enabled me to make the place I live in mine.

Because I rent, I asked the landlord if I could paint, and he said, "Whatever makes you comfortable." My living room walls were all pale yellow, but I sponge-painted the one wall above the fireplace a robin-egg's blue, to match one of the colors in a quilt my sister made for me; the quilt is draped over half of my lime green futon. The blue also matches a poster-sized picture of irises that hangs on the wall and a glass lamp given to me by my grandmother. My dining room chairs are a similar color.

In my living room, I also have a purple recliner and a smaller multicolored upholstered chair that matches my rug. In the center of the living room is a large pine chest that doubles as a table and a storage space since it has deep drawers on either side. Some of my furniture is pretty old, but the futon, the quilt, some throw pillows, and a piece of fabric here and there brighten things up.

The built-in bookcases in the living room and dining room are packed with books I love, and I have photographs of my family in the living room, hanging on the wall over my piano in the dining room, and sitting on shelves. It's comforting to have my family around me, even when they are not physically present. I am fortunate to have many photographs of my close family members as well as pictures of my great grandparents and my great aunts and uncles, relatives who lived before my time.

Aside from photos, I have artwork, some of it made by my children and grandchildren, which is beautiful to me, in various places around the house as well as things like pottery, seashells, and knick-knacks.

I repainted the cupboards and woodwork in my kitchen a brilliant white, and I have plans to paint the walls, now a pale yellow like most of the living room, a brighter canary yellow. I have touches of red in my kitchen, including a throw rug and a set of kitchen knives with red handles. I also have some red and yellow potholders and ceramic roosters with touches of red and yellow, souvenirs I bought when I took a trip to the Azores with my sister and grandson several years ago.

I even took the time to decorate my tiny bathroom. I found a lovely and unusual shower curtain with grape and black flowers, colors that match my bathroom towels and rug, and I have various colored glass bottles for my beauty potions and lotions.

My bedroom is the most special place in my house, for there I not only sleep, but also I read, write, think, and dream. My sheets are purple, my bedclothes yellow and purple, my two favorite colors. I have a bookcase with my favorite books, and a table and chair for my computer. Above my bed is a Navaho Prayer Flag, and on one of the walls is a framed picture of a lone wolf, which a dear friend gave to me during a time when I was having many dreams about wolves. Next to the wolf is a dreamcatcher.

An old dresser I found sits in the hallway because it didn't fit in my bedroom, and I painted it purple to match the colors on my bed. On it sits a canvas painting of the Virgin of Guadalupe. "She" is important to me, as I will mention in a later chapter. Several beeswax candles surround her.

My house is, as one friend said, "colorful." Another friend said, "Your house looks like you." Although I've given you only a glimpse into my living space, I want to say that decorating, to help make your space beautiful to you, if it is not already, may help cheer you up. Just using paint here and there made my house brighter. I have found some of my favorite things at thrift stores and garage sales, so decorating does not have to be an expensive project. When I am extremely depressed, I let my house go, but most of the time I find caring for my home very enjoyable.

I want to mention my yard because it, too, reflects me. Outside I have a small patio, and in the flowerbeds surrounding the patio, I have many different kinds of potted ferns (my favorite plant), many different colored roses (my favorite flower), as well as pansies, marigolds, and more. I have a few tomato plants growing in a small raised bed. On my patio, I have a small table and a few chairs because I often go in the backyard to sit, read, and drink my morning coffee. Caring for my small garden also brings me pleasure.

Whether you own your house or rent, most likely your home is where you spend a great deal your time. Surrounding yourself with colors that you like, mementos that are important to you, and things that bring you pleasure can make your house more comfortable and inviting. Whether you like elaborate or simple, unconventional or traditional, making your house your home may help bring some solace in your distress.

Moving Out of My Comfort Zone

I added this paragraph at the last minute, during which time I was editing my book and after going through a difficult major depressive episode. During that time, I realized I had to do something more to care for myself, so I promised myself I would do one thing each month, which would take me out of my comfort zone. Because I am an introvert, for me this means doing something social with people I don't already know. So, I decided for the first month to try a support group again because the one support group I went to was so many years ago and maybe I didn't give it a chance. I haven't tried this yet, but it's on my agenda.

We all have different gifts, hobbies, interests—things that bring us pleasure. Some of you reading this may enjoy walking, or hiking, or writing, like I do. But some of you may enjoy golfing, or playing a musical instrument, or singing, or cooking, or swimming, or dancing, or painting, or fishing. Pursuing a hobby or a project, or trying out some new thing that you've always wanted to do (or even trying out something entirely "different" that you're not sure you will like), can be the first step for flying out of that jar. Activities that bring meaning and/or pleasure into my life have been the first line of defense in managing my own depression.

6 ~ Mania

Much Madness is divinest Sense —
To a discerning Eye —
Much Sense — the starkest Madness —
'Tis the Majority —
In this, as all, prevail —
Assent — and you are sane —
Demur — you're straightway dangerous —
And handled with a Chain —

—Emily Dickinson,
Poem 620

I am not an expert on mania as I have only experienced one manic episode. But I grew up with my brother, who was three years older than I, and I saw him in many full-blown manic states.

When Curtis was only fourteen (up until then he appeared to be a "normal" kid), he became manic, seemingly out of the blue. First he stole a basketball from a store (he had not stolen anything before); then he ran away from home. The

49

police eventually picked him up because they thought he was high on drugs, but he eventually landed in the mental ward of a local hospital in a straitjacket, and on Thorazine, initially diagnosed with schizophrenia. The doctors told my parents that they had given him enough Thorazine to kill anyone my brother's size, but my brother lay in a straitjacket, full of Thorazine and still talking a mile a minute, as high as a kite.

According to the fifth edition of the *Diagnostic and Statistical Manual of Mental Disorders* (*DSM-5*), the criteria for a Manic Episode include the following:

A. A distinct period of abnormally and persistently elevated, expansive, or irritable mood and abnormally and persistently increased goal-directed activity or energy, lasting at least 1 week and present most of the day, nearly every day (or any duration if hospitalization is necessary).

B. During the period of mood disturbance and increased energy or activity, three (or more) of the following symptoms (four if the mood is only irritable) are present to a significant degree and represent a noticeable change from usual behavior.

   ❖ Inflated self-esteem or grandiosity.

   ❖ Decreased need for sleep (e.g., feels rested after only 3 hours of sleep).

   ❖ More talkative than usual or pressure to keep talking.

   ❖ Flight of ideas or subjective experience that thoughts are racing.

❖ Distractibility (i.e., attention too easily drawn to unimportant or irrelevant external stimuli), as reported or observed.

❖ Increase in goal-directed activity (either socially, at work or school, or sexually) or psychomotor agitation (i.e., purposeless non-goal-directed activity).

❖ Excessive involvement in pleasurable activities that have a high potential for painful consequences (e.g., engaging in unrestrained buying sprees, sexual indiscretions, or foolish business investments).

C. The mood disturbance is sufficiently severe to cause marked impairment in social or occupational functioning or to necessitate hospitalization to prevent harm to self or others, or there are psychotic features.

D. The episode is not attributable to the physiological effects of a substance (e.g., a drug of abuse, a medication, or other treatment) or a general medical condition.[7]

Reprinted with permission from the Diagnostic and Statistical Manual of Mental Disorders, Fifth Edition (Copyright ©2013). American Psychiatric Association.

The drug that my brother was taking, Thorazine, is sometimes prescribed for schizophrenia, and the manic phase of manic-depression, but it does not seem to be the drug of choice for either of these any more. Thorazine did not help lessen my brother's manic symptoms, and it was not until he was prescribed lithium, many years later, that any drug seemed to help him. My brother alternated between deep depression (where he stayed in bed all day) and full-blown manic attacks.

He was committed to Stockton State Hospital for about five years, beginning when he was fifteen years old. He came home when he was depressed, and he remained hospitalized when he was manic.

The use of lithium for the treatment of mental disorders was discovered in the nineteenth century, but it wasn't until 1970 that the Food and Drug Administration (FDA) approved lithium for use in America; the United States became the fiftieth country to approve it. Lithium is an element. Its name comes from *lithos*, the Greek word for "stone," so named because trace amounts of lithium are found in igneous rocks.

As a psychiatric medication, lithium is a mood-stabilizing drug used primarily in the treatment of bipolar disorder. Although lithium is prescribed less often than it once was, mainly due to the advent of so many newer drugs, Willem A. Nolen, in the *International Journal of Bipolar Disorders*, concludes that "lithium should be recommended as the single referred first-line drug in the long-term treatment of bipolar disorder."[8] Lithium is effective in preventing mania, and it worked for my brother. And although other studies show that lithium is less effective in preventing depression, it has lessened my day-to-day depression significantly.

Like most psychiatric drugs, the exact mechanisms of how lithium works are unknown, but it seems that its ultimate effect is to restore the balance of certain neurotransmitters in the brain. Ironically, lithium is not approved by the FDA for treatment of major depression, although the markers for bipolar depression and major depression are identical (the underlying causes of each disorder are thought to be different). And, even though study after study shows that lithium substantially reduces the risk of suicide in depressed patients, writers on this subject agree that lithium is not approved for use in major depression or as an augmentation strategy for major depression (adding lithium to another prescribed medication or medications) because of one certain thing: money. Studies showing the benefits of lithium as an augmenting agent were done many years ago, and lithium is cheap and has been available in generic form for years, so there has been no financial incentive for pharmaceutical companies to do the studies to gain FDA approval. Nevertheless, I am certain that lithium would have helped me with depression before my one manic episode in the same way that it worked for me afterward.

Lithium allowed my brother to live a somewhat normal life. On his meds, my brother was a charming man with a wonderful sense of humor and an almost child-like simplicity. He met a woman at a hospital support group and eventually married her, and although he never drove a car or worked, he remained relatively stable for many years. I could write a whole book about my brother's trouble with his Bipolar I disorder, but suffice it to say that when taking lithium coupled with another antipsychotic medication (Haldol) plus another drug to offset the side effects of the Haldol (Haldol gave my brother petite-mal seizures), he was stable. However, if he stopped the lithium, which he did on more than on occasion, he would experience a full-blown manic attack within days.

On one notable occasion, Curtis, off his meds, threw a rock at his wife's psychiatrist because he thought that her psychiatrist was not helping her. The doctor pressed charges—assault with a deadly weapon (the rock)—and my brother ended up in the Nevada County Jail. (He was about twenty-nine at the time.) Now, my brother was a big, strong, man on his meds or off, but when off his meds and mad, he was like a raging bull. In jail, he bent the bars of his jail cell with his bare hands and was then transferred to Folsom State Prison because the Nevada County Jail did not have the facilities to manage him.

I found out about all of this when I got a phone call from the prison psychiatrist, who further told me that my brother had run out into the prison yard and was almost killed for doing so. The doctor and I discussed my brother, and I told the doctor about my brother's diagnosis and his medications. The doctor, to his credit, seemed genuinely concerned. He put Curtis back on his meds, and my brother's moods were stabilized once again. Once stabilized, he was transferred back to jail. He spent about three months in jail, and during this time he tried unsuccessfully to kill himself by drinking a bottle of shampoo.

After my episode of mania, it took me a full year to agree to take lithium. I wasn't afraid of the drug, even though my brother died, at fifty-seven, from complications from the drugs he was taking. I was afraid of taking lithium because that would mean, in my mind at least, that I was mentally ill. Doctors now monitor lithium levels very carefully through blood tests, and I began taking lithium in my late forties (my brother was in his early twenties when he first began taking it; he was taking more than twice the amount of lithium that I now take). The only side effect I have from taking lithium is a fine tremor, most noticeable in my hands.

After my manic episode, which occurred in May of 1998, when I was forty-seven years old, I told the dean at the college where I was employed the truth about why I needed to cancel summer school, and she told me "not to tell anyone"; she could easily find another teacher to take my classes. She felt there should be no written disclosure of the nature of my illness because it might negatively affect me in the future, although I am sure her concerns were unfounded. Obviously, the stigma of mental illness is powerful, and the negative stereotype associated with it affects us all.

Before my manic episode, I had been depressed. I was under a great deal of stress, as I mentioned before. I was leaving a fourteen-year relationship, including leaving the house that Scott and I had built together; my therapist was going to Europe; and my sleep had been erratic, if nonexistent, for three days. I was taking Ambien for sleep, and I still wonder whether or not that drug played a part in my manic episode, for Ambien is now known to cause hallucinations in some people. (Ambien was definitely not helping me sleep.) I was not taking any other medications at the time, and I was not drinking (I hardly ever drink).

I wrote the following journal entry a few days before my episode:

> I have left Scott in body and soul—we don't sleep together any more—haven't in two years, and we speak only in passing. He knows I am halfway out the door, but we haven't talked about why I haven't left yet, and I know *he* would never leave. In fact, we don't talk about anything anymore, at least not any significant thing, certainly not anything that has to do with my feelings anyway. I have tried so many times to talk to him, but he refuses to talk or just leaves. I make him angry.

> When I first met Scott, I was so infatuated. He was as extroverted as I was introverted. He was handsome, witty, articulate, charming as well as a good mix between a professional and a blue-collar worker. But as the years have passed, our opposite natures seem to collide rather than complement one another.

He is an outrageous flirt even in places like restaurants where waitresses are drawn to his "golden tongue" and flashing blue eyes, and he is not willing to compromise that one annoying trait though I have compromised so much for the sake of our relationship. I go to his race car events, I socialize with all of his car friends, and I've long accepted the fact that I come in second to his love affair with certain kinds of beautiful automobiles.

I am so depressed, but I don't know how to leave. How do I open that side of myself that needs opening? Where is it? I can't stay this stuck forever. More than anything, I pray for a spiritual experience, something truly life changing that will take me away from the dead-end place where I now live.

Two days after writing this, I told Scott I was leaving. And, about a week later, I had my first, and so far my only, manic attack.

Scott had left by himself on a road trip to let me move my things out without him being there. My two-year-old grandson was staying with me. I woke up in the morning, after sleeping very little, and my world had literally changed. For one, everything was clothed in vibrant brilliant color, and my energy level was elevated, expansive, high. I cleaned the house, listened to music, drew pictures, cooked, took up projects I had started years ago. Because what was happening to me was so unlike what I had seen with my brother, it never occurred to me that I was having a manic episode. Truly, I believed I was having some kind of spiritual experience, the kind I had prayed for in my journal. I did not have pressured speech; I did not engage in "spending sprees, sexual indiscretions, or foolish business investments." Mostly I just stayed at home with my grandson.

Positively, I began building an altar, a project I had wanted to do for years (my Portuguese grandmother had always had one in her home, and two of my Mexican-American friends had beautiful altars in their home as well). I built it with a small statue of Mary in the center, and it was adorned with beautiful multicolored flowered cloth, candles, all kinds of beads, flowers, and small pictures of people whom I loved. Negatively, much of the anger I had toward Scott that I had repressed for so long came rushing to the surface, and I got a bunch of his stuff together, mostly pictures of cars and racetrack memorabilia, and I dumped all of it into the burn barrel we had outside, and I set fire to it.

During this time a friend came by, and she sensed that something was very wrong. She seemed especially concerned about the altar and that I had some of the windows in the house open (the main part of the house was on the second story), and she was afraid that my young grandson might fall out. In all fairness to myself, there was nothing dangerous about the windows being opened; they were mostly always open. I watched my grandson carefully, and I was perfectly capable of taking care of him.

Anyway, she called my therapist, who was about to leave for Europe, and he, in turn, called the police in order for them to do a wellness check. When the police arrived, I was more than shocked. I lived out in the country on seven acres, and I seldom had visitors. When the police came to the door, I, of course, let them in. We talked for a bit, but finding nothing amiss, they left.

Needless to say, this police visit infuriated me, and I called my therapist and left message after message, giving him a piece of my mind for calling the police. I remember not answering the phone when he returned my calls, and I remember hanging up on him more than once. However, we finally did talk, and he advised me to go and see my physician in Sutter Creek, where I lived at the time.

I drove my grandson home to his mother, my daughter, in Sacramento that evening. Then, the next day, I went to see my physician. I waited about two hours in the waiting room because I did not have a scheduled appointment. My doctor talked with me; then he sent me home. Although I was aware that something was "different," it was not apparently evident to the police or to my doctor. Again, my episode was very unlike what I had seen with my brother; I surely was not talking fast like I had seen him do. I was not acting bizarre in public, and I had the patience to wait two hours in the doctor's waiting room, keeping to myself the whole time.

Nevertheless, my energy level remained very high, and my thoughts were racing as well. When I drove my grandson home (it was evening), I saw white halos around the cars on the road and colors illuminating the darkness. I later wrote a poem called "Streaming Rainbow Nights" as a result of that drive. And, my perception was just off about certain things, although I was not aware of it at the time. For example, I thought, for some reason, that David was coming to see me, but I had little reason to believe he made home visits. He had told me he was leaving for Europe, but I didn't believe him, and I waited for more than three days for him to show up.

The most prominent feature of my manic episode is the hardest to describe. A psychiatrist might call this feature a "flight of ideas," but it was certainly more than this. It was an ability to combine concepts and ideas, readings, pictures, beliefs, feelings about people, and external events into one coherent and marvelous whole. The world was teeming with color, beauty, and connections—I saw everything as interconnected.

In *Touched with Fire, Manic-Depressive Illness and the Artistic Temperament*, Dr. Kay Redfield Jamison states that "manic patients . . . tend to exhibit pronounced *combinatory* [emphasis mine] thinking."[9] She further says that "The increased quantity and speed of thoughts may exert an effect on the qualitative aspects of thought as well; that is, the sheer volume of thought can produce unique ideas and associations."[10] Of course, the focus of her book is famous artists and how "madness" contributed to their artistry. Among the artists Jamison writes about are Byron, Tennyson, Shelley, Coleridge, and Ruskin; the list goes on and on.

My own "madness" felt like a marriage of my conscious and unconscious minds as well as a union of my intellect, my feelings, my intuition, and my physical senses. Unfortunately, I wrote only a few pages in my journal during this time. But I drew with colored pens and pastels. My favorite drawing is of a pulsating circle in the center of the page, colored blue with zig-zagging lines, the circle intersected by one black vertical line and one black horizontal line, forming a cross. Two black diagonal lines intersect the cross, all equidistant from each other. One side of the circle, in the blank spaces framed by the lines, I colored yellow; the other side I colored pink. On the top of the circle in the blank spaces framed by the lines, I colored purple; the bottom, green.

Truthfully, it looks like a monstrance, an ostensorium, minus the stand. I had seen this vessel, used in Roman Catholic churches to display the host in ceremonies like the Benediction of the Blessed Sacrament, many times in my life. The circle could be the host, the lines like crosses, rays of the sun, which the lines in a monstrance literally represent. Surely there were religious undertones and overtones to my whole manic episode. But, when I "painted" this picture, I wasn't really conscious of what I was drawing; this image just came pouring out of me.

After about four or five days, my expansive mood began to subside, but very slowly, and I began to sleep through the night. Remnants from my manic episode, especially a higher-than-normal energy level, persisted for about two weeks. During this time, I was able to find a place to rent in nearby Amador City, about five miles away from my Sutter Creek home. A friend helped me move my belongings out in his truck. While getting the last of my things from what had been Scott's and my house, Scott came home. And although he was furious that I had burned some of his car-related treasures (in fact, he had made a call to my therapist as well), we talked a little. He owed me about $40,000 for the equity I had paid into our house, and because he didn't have the cash to pay me back, he signed the title of his new Range Rover over to me until he could come up with the money.

A week or so later, I received a letter from my so-called friend who had called my therapist, informing me that she had called him as well as telling me that she could not deal with me, meaning my mental illness. I never heard from her again.

Another so-called friend, one whom I considered my best friend before my episode, also wrote me a letter after she found out about my manic attack. Her letter indicated that she was bowing out of our friendship; I was just not the person she had thought I was. After that, I would see her around school occasionally (she was a teacher also), and although I would go out of my way to say hello, I guess I was now branded with a *crazy* sign. Of course, these women were not really my friends after all. When David got back from Europe, we talked extensively about what had happened, many times. He referred me to two different psychiatrists (I didn't like the first one) to "get another opinion." Both said that I had certainly had a manic episode. I felt comfortable talking with the second psychiatrist, so I asked him about why my manic episode was so unlike my brother's. He told me that mania can manifest itself very differently in different people. So, I decided I just had to live with that.

It is estimated that 5.5 million Americans suffer from bipolar disorder. It typically begins in adolescence or early adulthood, but it can start as late as age forty or fifty. A person can have just one manic episode (like I did) or many (like my brother). Finding the correct diagnosis may be difficult. A survey conducted by the National Depressive and Manic-Depressive Association (DMDA) found that "69 percent" of patients with bipolar disorder "were misdiagnosed," and "Over one third waited 10 years or more before receiving an accurate diagnosis."[11]

I was prescribed lithium because of my one manic attack, not because of my lifelong problems with depression. However, once I began taking it, I felt my depression decrease significantly in less than a week. As I said previously, my reticence to take this medication was based primarily on my fear of being labeled as mentally ill. But, I now know that what others may think, or what even you may think about your own psychiatric diagnosis, pales in comparison to what is the very most important thing—alleviating your suffering, helping yourself to feel better.

7 ~ Trouble (Anxiety, Worry)

> Double, double toil and trouble;
> Fire burn, and cauldron bubble.
>
> —William Shakespeare,
> *Macbeth*

The power of the often-quoted passage from *Anna Karenina* by Russian writer Leo Tolstoy, "All happy families are alike; each unhappy family is unhappy in its own way,"[12] lies, for me, in his notice of the particularity of unhappy families. For although strong relationships, mutual support, and good communication are qualities of all happy families, suffering of every stripe and color—poverty, alcoholism, drug abuse, mental and physical illness, unresolved or unconscious childhood issues played forward—may serve to break the bonds of relationships, weaken if not decimate support systems, and fracture communication in families that are not so happy. Each family member affects the other, and for average people to transcend difficult, if not unimaginable, calamities unscathed and without negatively affecting other family members is nearly impossible. With that being said, suffering, even in not-so-happy families, is not ubiquitous.

After the onset of my brother's illness, I would characterize my family as an unhappy one, even though my sisters, much younger than I am, may remember these times differently. My father was a car painter; my mother a housewife. My brother Curtis was three years my senior. I have two sisters; my sister Jenna is seven years younger than I, and my younger sister Molly is ten years my junior.

When I was ten, a year and a half before my brother got sick, in 1961, my uncle Sonny, my mother's brother, died in an automobile accident when he was thirty-two. Not only were my mother and her brother extremely close, but also Sonny was my favorite uncle. I remember many beautiful dresses he bought for me, and once, for my birthday, he gave me a tin can full of marbles, about one hundred of them, each individually wrapped in colored tissue paper, each tied with a ribbon. My uncle and I had a special bond, and, like me, he was sensitive, with an artistic and aesthetic bent. I mention Sonny here because the death of my uncle was the first major loss I experienced in my childhood. Other losses would soon follow.

When my brother got sick at fourteen, it tore my parents' marriage apart. So little was known about mental illness in the 1960s, and my parents were working-class people who, I am sure, had little idea about what was happening. My mother had a high school education, and my father went into the navy at sixteen. My parents went through school together and married when they both were twenty. I have a picture of them in their sixth-grade class, my mother looking like a young woman already, with a long plaid skirt and a crisp white cotton blouse. My father, shorter than my mother at the time, is wearing a sweatshirt, smiling rakishly at the camera, looking like a miniature James Dean.

The most difficult thing about growing up in my household can be partially expressed with the words, "Children are to be seen and not heard." What I mean by this is that in my family, at least for my brother and me, we never really talked with our parents about any significant thing, certainly not our feelings. They, in turn, never talked with us. When my brother was going "crazy," he was scary, loud, and strange, so unlike the brother I had known only a few years before, but no one ever talked to me about what was going on. I remember a time when I was eleven, sitting in a chair in the kitchen, shaking, waiting with my parents for a phone call from Curtis (or the police) because Curtis had run away. When the phone finally rang, my brother would at first talk only to me. I don't remember what he said or what I said. What I remember is that no one ever talked with me about what was going on.

When my brother was committed to Stockton State Hospital, I visited him every other weekend with my parents and with my grandmother on alternate weekends. But no one really talked to me about what was going on. And when my brother would come home for a week or two during the depressive phase of his manic-depressive illness, when he would just sleep all day, still no one talked to me about what was going on.

My mother was a beautiful Portuguese woman with dark brown hair and big brown eyes. My mother, I am certain, suffered from an undiagnosed and untreated depressive disorder.

First of all, I don't think she ever got over her brother's death. After Sonny died, she never seemed really happy. And although I am very sure that she loved her children, she did not know how to show it. I do not remember ever being held or hugged by her as a child, but I do have some pictures of myself as a baby, sitting on her lap.

My mother only had a few friends whom she talked to on the phone once in a while, but aside from her mother, her father, my father, and her children, and of course Sonny, when he was alive, she was very much alone. Because she was legally blind, she never drove a car, so when my father was at work, she was stuck at home all day. My mother died at forty-four when I was twenty-one. I wish she were alive today. I wish I could talk with her about all those difficult years.

My brother and I were close to my mother's mother. Our grandmother came to visit us a little too often, as much as every other day, which caused friction between my mother and her. Grandma had only a sixth-grade education, so I am sure that my brother's illness was difficult for her to understand; nevertheless, she loved her grandchildren unconditionally. When I became depressed myself, even though I was close to my grandmother, I never spoke to her about what I was going through. Talking to a family member about my feelings is something I would never have thought of doing.

My father was a tall, handsome man of English and Italian heritage. He had thick dark curly black hair and a strong, but slender build. Silent and reserved much of the time, he, nevertheless, made friends easily and people seemed to be drawn to him. My father had a reflective streak, and after dinner, I remember his listening to records, to those singers who are now considered the great classic country artists—Hank Williams,

Senior; Merle Haggard; Waylon Jennings. I remember my father sitting in his easy chair, just listening, hour after hour. Although I hated this music in my teenage years, having grown up during the fantastic music revolution of the 1960s with the great folk, blues-rock, and rock bands, ironically, today, country music is my favorite.

My father, the center of his biological family, was the oldest among five siblings, and his two brothers and two sisters looked up to him. My aunt June and my uncle Will (my father's sister and her husband) and my cousins would come to our house to visit every weekend, and these are some of my most wonderful childhood memories. Sadly, however, my father did not really seem close to my brother, and, even today, I do not understand why. I have wondered if jealousy over displacement was a factor, as my brother was the first-born and the only boy in our family. But this is pure speculation, my need to find answers to questions I still have.

I do not remember my father teaching my brother to fish, something my father loved to do; I do not remember my brother and my father playing baseball, or "catch," or board games, or any of the things that many fathers and sons do together. Certainly, they didn't talk together about anything of significance. The only thing my brother and father shared was their love of bowling. Both my father and my brother played in bowling leagues, and both were very good bowlers, with bowling averages in the 200s. I remember one special Christmas when my brother was about eleven. He received a gift of a bowling game from my parents, with life-sized bowling pins and balls. We set the bowling game up in our living room, and my brother and I played for hours.

More demonstrative than my mother, my father expressed

his love through kidding and teasing us, and we all, including my brother, enjoyed this interaction with him. But overall, we were a "no-touch" family. To be fair, physical affection did not seem all that common in families of this generation and earlier, at least from accounts of other friends my age and from the account of my mother's cousin, with whom I have talked at length.

My father remarried shortly after my mother's death, and I danced with him—my father was a great dancer—at his wedding reception. Unlike anything I had ever experienced before with my father, our dancing together remains one of my most heartfelt memories. I would love to dance with my father again, but more than this, I would love to talk with him about all those difficult years. Like my mother, my father died prematurely, when he was fifty-seven.

When my brother got sick, relations grew more strained between my father and my brother and extremely strained in our household. I remember a great deal of tension in the house, so much so that when I would walk home from junior high school, right before I would open the door, I prepared myself for seeing everyone on the floor, dead. The prospect of this happening may have been nonexistent, but this is how my twelve- and thirteen-year-old mind registered the pressure. And even though negative emotions were not expressed very much in our household, certainly not in any overt way like yelling or fighting, the tension was there. My household felt like powder keg sitting close to a fire.

After my brother's illness, the rift between my brother and my father grew deeper. And my mother, being a mother, could not understand my father's seemingly lack of feelings toward her only son. I write "seemingly" because I do believe that, deep down, my father loved my brother. Nevertheless, I have a letter that my mother wrote to herself during this time, which I found in the pocket of her bathrobe after her death, expressing her frustration and her anger toward my father. My parents may not have fought or yelled at each other, but their relationship was broken. Today, I can only imagine how confusing and overwhelming my brother's illness must have been for my parents. I can only imagine how much they suffered because of it.

My parents did not really read books, so I don't know how they learned of author Thomas Anthony Harris or how meeting him came about. All of this happened, of course, before the Internet, that wonderful tool that allows us to research anything both easily and quickly. But, somehow, my parents learned of Harris's book *I'm OK, You're OK*, first published in 1969, and they met with this author. And although I'm not an expert on the "I'm OK, You're OK" philosophy, transactional analysis, it is the theory that unproductive or counterproductive interactions, "transactions," can be made right through talk therapy, especially family group therapy. I do know that this was before doctors learned that manic-depression was a biological illness with a genetic basis. I know for sure that psychotherapy alone would not have helped my brother.

Even though nothing much seemed to come out of this meeting with this author, I mention it here because I believe my parents did everything they could do, under the circumstances and given their limitations, to find the answer to my brother's illness. At this time, the stigma of mental illness was huge—much greater than it is today—and my brother's illness and hospitalization was a family secret. There was no larger support system available to our family, and my parents were very much alone in trying to understand and cope with the radical changes in my brother's life and their own.

Writing about my parents has been the most difficult thing about writing this book, and I do not mean to disparage them in any way. All families have issues, and often those issues are the result of what preceded them and are, unfortunately, carried forward. Most of us do the very best we can, given our limitations. As I see it, our job is to examine the forces that led us to where we are for the purpose of understanding ourselves better, "accepting the things we cannot change," and then letting go. Blaming anyone or any one thing is tiring and unproductive. There is always enough blame to go around. As Fernando Pessoa so elegantly writes, "We are all equal in our capacity for error and suffering."[13]

Although my family's troubles stick out in my mind, I remember many wonderful times. Among the best of my childhood experiences were our camping trips. Every year, when Memorial Day weekend rolled around, which coincided with my birthday, we would set off on our first camping trip. We camped often during the summer and always on my dad's yearly vacations. I remember camping at Icehouse Reservoir, Pardee Dam, and Topaz and Loon Lakes, all within a hundred and fifty miles of Sacramento. One of my best childhood memories is camping for a week at Lassen National Park, before my brother's illness and before my sisters were born. However, during one of these family camping trips, many years after the Lassen vacation, tragedy struck one sunny morning on the Fourth of July.

My father and mother, my two little sisters (my brother was in the hospital), my aunt June and uncle Will and my cousins Carolyn, Mary, and Mark, as well as another family (friends of my parents) and Laurie and Jack, their two kids, went car camping together at Salt Springs (I remember the name, but nothing else). Five of us kids—myself, my cousin Mary, her older sister Carolyn, and Laurie and Jack—decided to take a hike, and on our way back, we decided to take a shortcut to our camp. And foolishly, foolishly, we decided to run down a hill. There were, of course, trees at the bottom of the hill, and my cousin Mary, just seven years old, struck her head on a tree and died, almost instantly.

Laurie, a year younger than I, ran down the hill first, followed by my cousin Mary. I remember Laurie screaming at me, screaming to come down now, that Mary was hurt. After I ran down the hill, I saw Mary lying on her back, unconscious, a tiny stream of blood trickling from her mouth. Someone ran to get the adults, and they began artificial respiration and continued to give Mary artificial respiration all the way to the hospital. Later, a doctor told my aunt and uncle that if my cousin had struck her head on something as hard as that tree in exactly the same way, even if it had happened in the hospital, he could not have saved her. The doctor also told my aunt and uncle that Mary had likely died seconds after she hit the tree.

Because I was thirteen and the oldest, because I should have known better than to run down a steep hill where there were trees at the bottom, because I should have known better than to let children who were younger than I run down this hill, I still, today, feel a terrible guilt concerning this tragedy. This event runs back through my mind, especially during the summer months, and I wonder if my recurring summer depression is what psychologists call an "Anniversary Reaction" relating to that tragic Fourth of July.

Looking back at my cousin's death today, I wish my parents had let the kids (at least Mary's older sister Carolyn, and me) go to the funeral. Although that didn't happen, I think it may have helped us heal more quickly. Of course, my parents never talked about the events of that Fourth of July with me. I had been there, so, perhaps they assumed, that was enough. What I remember about the time after Mary's death is that my aunt June, Mary's mom, was sick for many weeks, and she did not come to our house for quite a while. I was close with Carolyn, Mary's sister, three years younger than I, so we comforted each other by talking and talking and talking. This incident made us very close, and we remained so until I got married, and then we went our separate ways.

Certainly every family has its tragedies, and many families experience tragedies much worse than what I have related here. Suicides, homicides, illnesses, accidents of every kind, and the simple fact that we are aware of our impending deaths and of the impending deaths of others whom we love are but a fraction of what human beings endure. But for me, my uncle's death, my brother's illness, my parents' growing estrangement, and then my cousin's death, all coming close to the same time, certainly took a toll on me. These all may have been latent triggers for the depressive episodes that consumed so much of my life later on. I was thirteen and grown.

Once my brother got sick, I began to worry, and I worried incessantly. I remember bargaining with God, telling him I would do this, that, or another thing—I don't remember what, exactly—if he would only make my brother well. And although I still love the mountains, I am overly cautious and aware, wherever I am, that disaster could strike at any time.

I worry still, and I worry about many things. Sometimes I think that worry and anxiety are equally as painful as depression, and for me, they are certainly a part of it. When I worry, I am anxious and overwrought. I feel vulnerable and unprotected. I feel a sense of foreboding and alarm. Most of all, I feel afraid. Certainly, the internal dimensions of anxiety are different for each of us. But for me, it's like there is some kind of darkness roaring inside of me, and it's hard to make it stop. I am unsure of how much of my worrying nature today stems from my depressive illness and how much stems from these various childhood traumas.

While doing some research for this book, I put the words *worry and anxiety* into my web browser and came up with over 60 million hits in under a second. I perused about twenty articles that focused on self-help for worriers and read about all kinds of productive things, from eating dark chocolate and drinking chamomile tea to exercise, meditation, and various other kinds of relaxation techniques. But out of everything I read, the words that spoke to me the most concerning worry and anxiety were, "just stop." Once I realize I am on that unproductive merry-go-round ride, just flipping the switch may be the simplest way to avoid excessive worry.

I was married once, at nineteen, and my marriage lasted for seven years. I gave birth to my son, Jeremy, when I was twenty-one; Ann, my daughter, was born three years later. My greatest life's regret is that I, like my mother, was a depressed mother, so my children did not get half of what they deserved from me. I had never even heard of the word depression until I was in my late twenties or early thirties, although in my freshman year at college, in my first composition class, I researched and wrote a ten-page paper on schizophrenia, my brother's initial diagnosis. I was still searching for answers.

Like my parents before me, I was not a physically demonstrative mother, although I did talk with my children. It wasn't until I took a child development course in my first year of college that I learned that children needed both physical affection and positive reinforcement—things that were oblivious to me before that time. Today, it seems preposterous that I did not simply know these things. One of my cousins says we all need to be given a book on parenting before we have children, so we can learn that our own parents may not be the best models for how to raise our children.

Sometime in my late twenties, I first saw a psychiatrist with my children for a few sessions because my son and daughter were fighting all of the time. Needless to say, these visits did not help because my children were unwilling to talk with her. Fortunately, the fighting problem seemed to resolve on its own. However, this psychiatrist recognized my depression, and sometime later, in my early thirties, if I remember correctly, she prescribed different medications to help relieve it.

In the following years, first by this psychiatrist and then by others, I was prescribed various drugs to help relieve my depression. Some that I tried included the tricyclics Elavil and Nortriptyline, and later, many of the selective serotonin reuptake inhibitors (SSRIs), including Prozac, Celexa, Zoloft, and Effexor. I tried one atypical antidepressant drug, Wellbutrin, and then Lamictal (sometimes used for mood disorders). As I said previously, all of these drugs gave me side effects but little relief. Lamictal made me nauseous to the point of throwing up.

The side effects of almost any kind of drug are numerous. Some side effects are merely annoying; some are life threatening. I have never taken any of the atypical antipsychotic drugs, drugs like Zyprexa, Risperdal, Latuda, and Abilify, which are sometimes used to treat bipolar disorder. Although these newer antipsychotic drugs seem to have a lower risk of tardive dyskinesia—a side effect I find unacceptable—than older anti-psychotic drugs, this noxious side effect is a particular fear of mine because my brother suffered from tardive dyskinesia, and this condition may be permanent.

Tardive dyskinesia (TD) presents with involuntary movements, especially in the face. This side effect may stop if the drug(s) causing it is stopped early enough, but it may not. TD is a possible, very serious side effect of several classes of psychiatric drugs—some of the tricyclics, some of the antidepressants, some of the antipsychotics—as well as some nonpsychiatric drugs. A doctor told me that the Haldol, rather than the lithium, caused my brother's involuntary movements, but perhaps it was both.

While doing research for this book, I was shocked to learn that lithium is included in various tables that list drugs for which TD is a possible side effect. After reading about this on the Internet, I literally ran to my medicine cabinet to see if TD was listed under the **Warning, Side Effects, or Precautions** on the insert that came with my lithium or to see if there was any language that might refer to TD such as "uncontrollable muscle movements." There was not, although there was the usual caveat, "This is not a complete list of possible side effects." One study did say that TD as a side effect of lithium was "rare."

However, if I had I known many years ago that lithium could, even remotely, cause tardive dyskinesia, would I have agreed to take it? Truthfully, probably not, as I am overcautious about almost everything. Will I stop taking it now? No, because I see little likelihood of something like that happening to me after all these years, and lithium continues to help me. For Curtis, the positive effects of his medications likely outweighed the negative side effects because without his medications, his moods were completely unstable. For Curtis, medication seemed to have been the better, of no real best, solution.

Although lithium has worked reasonably well for me, what has worked for me may not work for you. However, medication is one avenue to explore if you are suffering from bipolar disorder, or major depression, or any psychiatric illness for that matter. Needless to say, we must inform ourselves about what is out there and do our research—for it is our body, and our choice, whatever we may choose or choose not to do.

Unfortunately, although I have never used nonprescription drugs, and I seldom drink alcohol, I do sometimes smoke. I have never smoked as much as a half a pack of cigarettes a day; sometimes I smoke nothing, or only about one to three cigarettes a day; but I still have not been able to quit entirely. My dad, a heavy smoker, died of lung cancer, and my dad's sister, also a heavy smoker, and only a few years my senior, died of lung cancer as well. I know that we all do what makes us feel better, whether or not it is good for us. As I see it, we all have failings. We acknowledge them, and we continue to work on them.

My son is diagnosed with Bipolar I, and he has serious anxiety problems as well. He is extremely intelligent—brilliant, in fact—but like my brother, he has never been able to work because of the instability of his illness. Although he didn't finish high school, he reads, perhaps more than I do, and that is something we both share. Like me, he also writes. His depression, at times, can only be described as similar to mine—if not worse. Because I am a mother, I suffer when he is suffering. I know only too well what depression feels like. The expression, "A mother is only as happy as her most unhappy child" is true for me.

My daughter seems to have escaped the bipolar curse. Although she never finished college, she is bright and capable. And she has given me four wonderful grandchildren. She talks to her children, hugs her children, and tells them that she loves them. One of my grandsons has suffered from depression since he was a teenager. I can only pray that he hasn't inherited bipolar disorder from my side of the family; nevertheless, any kind of depression is terrible.

All of us, whether we are grandparents, parents, or children, have our own stories; they lie deep inside of us, whether we are storytellers, or writers, or not, and for most of us, our own life journey will entail trouble—sadness, worry, anxiety, stress. Almost all of us will experience trouble, except, perhaps, the great enlightened ones.

But life goes on. My therapist frequently alludes to the old Zen proverb, which speaks to the stream of life, whether we are enlightened or, like most of us, still struggling with our demons: "Before enlightenment, chopping wood and carrying water. After enlightenment, chopping wood and carrying water."

8 ~ Deep Water

I do not laugh, I do not cry;
I'm sweating out the will to die.

My past is sliding down the drain;
I soon will be myself again.

—Theodore Roethke,
The Collected Poems

W hen I see a homeless person on the street, wandering, suffering, lost, I see major depression in the flesh.

I would estimate that I have suffered from at least thirty major depressive episodes in my lifetime, about ten in the last sixteen years, since I began taking lithium, and many more before that time. At above level 5 on my water table numbering system, the water is not only creeping above my waist, but it is slowing approaching my head. Not only is it hard to move my legs, but also it is hard to move my arms, called "psycho-motor retardation" by psychiatrists. My mind is cloudy, fuzzy, scattered; my thoughts and my speech are slowing down; I can't find the right words to say what I mean, especially when I speak.

And although I generally have some problems sleeping, when in the middle of a major depressive episode, I *can* sleep, and I *want* to sleep, *all* of the time. I often cannot concentrate enough to read, even the most soothing music jars me, and other people's voices drum in my ears like random explosions of white noise.

As I mentioned in Chapter 5, during the course of finishing this book, I experienced a major depressive episode characterized by most of the symptoms listed in the chart from the *Diagnostic and Statistical Manual of Mental Disorders* (*DSM-5*) shown in Chapter 1. I became depressed in early summer, when the weather was in the high 80s and 90s (I often feel worse in the summer). This depressive episode lasted much longer than usual, more than eight weeks. I would estimate that my depression during this episode was between levels 5 and 7, with some days, and some hours of each day, registering at the lower or higher end.

It is difficult to assign a particular number to my depression once it is a 5 or above because the particulars are somewhat different every time. For example, sometimes, but not always, I am able to write a little or read a little. Sometimes, I can force myself to take a walk, but sometimes I can hardly move from the couch. However, I wrote in my journal one day during my most recent depressive episode, and this is what I wrote:

> My depression has been in the 5 to 7 range for about three weeks now. I am getting out of bed each morning, although several hours later than usual. Today and yesterday, I got up at around 10:30. It was a

struggle. Everything is a struggle. It's midafternoon, and I have already lost my keys three times somewhere in the house. I finally hooked the key chain around the doorknob. I try to read, but I have to go back and reread what I just read so many times, it's not worth it.

Janice e-mailed me, asking to go hiking, but I want to be by myself. David tells me I self-isolate when I am depressed. It's true. I forced myself to walk to the market today and bought some fruit. I am eating a little. I wrote some checks to pay some bills, made a few necessary phone calls. I washed the dishes.

But negative, fatalistic, and hopeless thoughts flood my mind, and as hard as I try to clear it, they come back as predictably as a boomerang. I am thinking too much, overthinking things, catastrophizing. Sometimes I just space-out, and sometimes I watch TV because it diverts my mind a little. I realize I am but the smallest particle in the large scheme of things, but I'm the one feeling what I'm feeling, and I'm feeling pretty awful. I need to stop thinking ahead. I need to focus on right here, right now.

Last night, I slept in my clothes. I plopped down on the bed about 10:00, but I did not have the energy to get up again to undress or wash my teeth. At least sleep gives me some relief.

Fortunately, my depression did not go above a 7. It seemed to have settled there, and then one day I was just feeling better, back to my more usual levels, between 2 and 4. This depressive episode may have been triggered by my worry concerning some problematic things that were happening in my family, but it's hard to say for sure. These same problems did not get worse or better, but I felt better nonetheless.

In Chapter 2, I wrote about how depression sometimes feels as if I am in a labyrinth, and I am trying with all my might to find a way out. This certainly applies when I am around a 5 on my water table scale, when the water is about up to my waist, and it is sometimes still applicable when my depression level hits 7. But once my depression climbs above a 7, the trying is over. Things I try but fail to do succeed only in frustrating me further.

Once during a deep depression, I remember sitting on my living room rug, trying to alphabetize my students' essays by last name before reading and grading them. I spent about fifteen minutes trying to alphabetize these papers, and I simply could not do it. I finally just burst out crying, from pure frustration, and then I threw them aside.

When in very deep water, I abandon things I cannot seem to do. I do not write; I abandon any kind of work I am doing; my plants go unwatered; my dishes sit in the sink or around the house, unwashed. I do not go out of the house to take a walk or to go shopping. I turn the ringer off on my phone. I do not look at my computer to browse the Internet or to answer or send e-mails. I do not wash my hair or bathe for days at a time. I generally eat very little. And, sometimes, I cancel my appointments with my therapist. I do this because I am so slowed down that I cannot seem to communicate effectively and because, sometimes, I feel I have nothing to say.

Writer Joan Didion shares the following words about herself from a psychiatric report written during a time when she was going through a mental crisis: "patient's responses are characteristic of those of individuals of high average or superior intelligence but she is now functioning intellectually in impaired fashion at barely average level."[14] During a major depressive episode, I am sure, for any of us, our IQ points inevitably drop.

Although when in the middle of a major depressive episode I may do very little except sleep, or sit in front of the television set, watching endless hours of TV, I have learned not to beat myself up about the things I simply cannot do. I *refuse* to feel guilty. I simply "let go," and I wait. I fight off the feelings of despair threatening to engulf me. For, I know, somewhere deep inside of me, "this too shall pass."

Portuguese author Fernando Pessoa writes about depression, without using that word, in his masterpiece *The Book of Disquiet*: "I have times of great stagnation . . . . In these periods of shadowy subsistence, I'm unable to think, feel or want. I can't write more than numbers and scribbles . . . I'm helpless. It's as if I were sleeping and my gestures, words and deliberate acts were no more than a peripheral respiration, the rhythmic instinct of some organism."[15]

This state of mind—**hell on earth**—may be impossible to understand for anyone who has not suffered a major depressive episode. Life seems to lose all purpose and meaning; willpower dissolves, like so many snowflakes in the sun, and immobility takes its place. I simply have no energy. I am *exhausted* in mind, body, and soul.

Because I live alone, and because I do not share with even my closest friends or family members that I am extremely depressed, it may, or may not, be worse for me. If I were living with someone, she or he could at least check up on me from time to time. On the other hand, most people, in my experience anyway, do not have much patience with a severely depressed person. They simply cannot tolerate what they see as *laziness, irritability, self-indulgence.*

Although my major depressive episodes usually last about two weeks, I am fortunate in that I may start feeling somewhat better after about ten days. As soon as my depression eases, I first take a shower and wash my hair; then, I wash the dishes. And, of course, when I was working full time, I go would go back to work. My major depressive episodes seem to resolve themselves; they are a cycle with a beginning and *thank God*, an ending.

Depression is a medical condition and a biological reality for millions of people worldwide. It is not a weakness. It is a fallacy that a lack of willpower or motivation is causing or exacerbating depression. Imaging studies have shown consistently that the left frontal portion of the brain becomes less active during depression. Depression is also associated with changes in how the pituitary gland and hypothalamus respond to hormone stimulation. Many medical theorists explain what they think is going on, biologically speaking, in a depressed person's brain, but various theories can be easily found on the Internet or in books, so I won't go into these further. However, I do want to talk about the most extreme outcome of depression, and that is suicide.

Poet Sylvia Plath completed suicide after two failed attempts. A short list among the hundreds of artists who have ended their own lives while suffering from depression-related illnesses includes John Berryman, Vachel Lindsey, Randell Jarrel, Ernest Hemingway, Vincent van Gogh and Virginia Woolf.

Woolf, author of *Mrs. Dalloway* (1925), *To the Lighthouse* (1927), and *A Room of One's Own* (1929), as well as twelve other books, suffered from manic-depressive illness. Before her suicide by drowning herself in the River Ouse in East Sussex, England, at age fifty-nine, she wrote a letter to her husband, leaving it for him on the mantle. It reads in part:

Dearest,

> I feel certain I am going mad again. I feel we can't go
> through another of those terrible times. And I shan't
> recover this time. I begin to hear voices, and I can't
> concentrate. So I am doing what seems the best thing
> to do. You have been in every way all that anyone
> could be. I don't think two people could have been
> happier till this terrible disease came. I can't fight
> any longer. I know that I am spoiling your life, that
> without me you could work. And you will I know.
> You see I can't even write this properly. I can't read .
> . . I can't go on spoiling your life any longer . . .[16]

According to an April 19, 1941, *New York Times* article,
"Her husband testified that Mrs. Woolf had been depressed for
a considerable amount of time." Certainly the war and the
Luftwaffe's bombing of Woolf's two London houses were con-
tributing factors to her depression. Her biographers surmise
there were other factors as well. Nevertheless, foreseeing another "terrible time" coupled with her belief that she was spoil-
ing her husband's life was more than Woolf could bear.

We all have our limitations and our breaking points. What
is for one person a divot in the road is for another a caldera.
Whether our various reactions to life's difficulties are the result
of nature, nurture, or both, or whether different people just
experience things differently, is hard to say. But difficult, if not
overwhelming, life circumstances, on top of a deep depression,
equal catastrophe. On May 28, 1941, Virginia Woolf filled her
jacket with stones and walked into the water near her home.
But, clearly, even before her death, she was already drowning.

Many other notable artists suffering from depressive illnesses have **attempted** suicide. A very short list includes Edgar Allan Poe, Joseph Conrad, Isak Dinesen, Herman Hesse, Eugene O'Neill, Mary Wollstonecraft, Hector Berlioz, Robert Shumann, Charles Parker, Paul Gauguin, and Dante Gabriel Rossetti. Of course, this ignores the millions of nonfamous depressives, ordinary people, who have ended, or will end, their own lives.

Both the National Institute of Health and Doctor Kay Redfield Jamison state that one in five persons suffering from bipolar disorder will complete suicide. Jamison elaborates, "From a slightly different perspective, at least two-thirds of those people who commit suicide have been found to have suffered from depressive or manic-depressive illness."[17] Jamison also says that because suicide is often looked at as being caused by external circumstances, existential angst, or volition, "the seriousness of manic-depressive illness as a potentially lethal medical condition is often overlooked." She further writes, "Suicide, for many who suffer from untreated manic-depressive illness, is as much 'wired' into the disease as myocardial infarction is for those who have occluded coronary arteries."[18]

The Centers for Disease Control reports that in 2013 (the most recent year for which full data are available), **41,149** suicides were reported in the United States, making suicide the tenth leading cause of death for Americans. Certainly, many of these Americans were depressed.

I have never attempted suicide. However, when I am deeply depressed, I do experience what psychiatry calls "suicidal ideation." This just seems to be a part and parcel of the illness. "Suicidal ideation" means entertaining the idea of suicide and thinking about how one might end his or her life. For me, when deeply depressed, suicidal thoughts come to me involuntarily and randomly. Sometimes I dwell on them; mostly I ignore them.

I know that if I were ever to commit suicide—although there is a very negligible chance of that happening—I would use a gun, or I would hike up into the mountains on a below-freezing day and just sit there until I lost consciousness. I have thought about suicide enough to know this. If I were planning to kill myself, I would try hard never to do something that possibly might *not* end my life. Pills, and other less reliable suicide methods, could result in a disability, with someone else then having to care for me. *That* is unthinkable. However, I realize that no suicide method is foolproof.

I once owned a gun. In fact, I owned a gun until very recently. The father of my former husband, a police officer, gave it to me sometime in the early 1970s. My former father-in-law believed that everyone should have a gun for self-protection. The gun that I owned was a .22 caliber Escort Model, a semiautomatic pistol, small enough to fit in my purse. But I always kept it hidden in the house on a top closest shelf, and no one else knew that it was there. For years at a time, I would forget about it; it only drifted into my mind occasionally when I was very depressed.

The last time I got extremely depressed, above a 7, about two years ago now, I did go to see my therapist, and it was the first time I told him that I owned a weapon. After talking with me about it at length, he told me to just "lose it," which I eventually did, but at the time I was too depressed to do this one simple thing. During that difficult time, certainly one of the worst depressive episodes I have ever experienced, David encouraged me to come to see him more frequently. I know he was worried about my "suicidal ideation" and even more concerned because he knew I owned a gun. I didn't go to see him more frequently, but he gave me his personal phone number "just in case." And although I didn't do that either (call him), it very much helped me to know that I *could*.

I would estimate there is less than a 1/2 of 1 percent chance that I would ever commit suicide. I personally think it is just too selfish. Suicide would not only end my life, but it could devastate the lives of people who love me. I would be setting a more-than-horrible example for my children and grandchildren. And, I could not see doing that to my therapist, after the hundreds of hours he has spent helping me. I am not a selfish person, and suicide seems very selfish to me.

I acknowledge that depressed individuals may think they are doing others a favor by taking their own lives. But I am certain that those who remain behind would strongly disagree. I know that if someone I loved committed suicide, I would be completely traumatized; it would be something I would never get over. Accepting a natural death is hard enough.

The best reason for me not to have a gun in the house concerns impulsivity. In one despairing instant, with a gun readily available, I could pick it up and end my life. Having a gun in the house is simply not worth the risk.

If you have suicidal thoughts and feel you may act on them, tell someone. Call your therapist or doctor or tell a close friend or trusted family member. If you have no one to talk with, call a suicide hotline. Death is inevitable for all of us, but a premature and unnecessary death is tragic. Feelings of suicide pass, and depressed feelings change, often for the better. Communicating your feelings may save your life. If you feel the world has abandoned you, don't abandon yourself!

9 ~ Spirituality

"Jesus Take the Wheel"
—Carrie Underwood

The country song "Jesus Take the Wheel" by Carrie Underwood concerns a young mother with a baby in her car, a mother who is low on "gas" and low on faith. Her car spins on the ice, out of control, on the way to her parents' house, and she finds herself stranded by the side of the road. The song's title is both a cry and a prayer. When things are overwhelming, it is both a positive and a natural thing to ask that our trials be lifted from our hands. In a crisis, we ask Jesus, God, what some call a Higher Power, within or without, for help. This is a most profound statement of faith.

There is much I cherish about the Catholic Church. I love the ritual. I love the Mass. I love the sacred ambiance of a

Catholic cathedral. Most of all, I love that Mary, the Mother God, is included, right there beside Jesus and the Father God. What I hate about Catholicism is the male hierarchy—deacon, priest, bishop, archbishop, cardinal, pope. Most of all, I hate Catholicism's denigration of women. Yes, women can serve as sponsors at Baptism and Confirmation; they can serve on parish councils and finance committees; they can read the Gospels; they can be ushers; they can even be Eucharistic ministers (serve Holy Communion). Nevertheless, women *cannot* be priests.

During my teenage years, I had planned on becoming a nun. I still have a response to a letter I wrote when I was sixteen, a response from the Missionary Sisters of the Immaculate Heart of Mary, dated October 25, 1967. I told the sisters in my letter that I was interested in the religious missionary life. In junior high school, my aunt gave me a subscription to *Maryknoll* magazine, and I read these magazines cover to cover. Maryknoll sisters were missionaries and nurses. That is what *I* wanted to be. In the response to my letter, Sister Agnes Marie, I.C.M., says in part, "Keep praying, dear Candy [my nickname], our Lord will lead you in the path He has planned for you. Keep close to the Blessed Mother of fair love; she will guard and protect you on your way to HIM." She also included a brochure, detailing their mission posts in Africa, the Philippines, Brazil, Guatemala, the West Indies, Formosa, and other parts of the world, worlds far away and wonderful, to my young mind.

Needless to say, I did not choose the religious life as my vocation, but my Catholic roots have stayed with me all of my life. I still sometimes go to church; I believe in the Sacraments; and I most definitely believe in prayer. I may not be a conventional Catholic, but I was taught, and I believe, that there are many ways, and many paths, to God. I believe, absolutely, what it says in Matthew 7:1: "Judge not, that ye be not judged."[19] This is my favorite biblical quote, although it is not really beautiful, ornate, or even profound. I am reminded of this quote every time I encounter someone's archaic attitude about matters like homosexuality, or homelessness, or mental illness.

I consider myself to be more of a spiritual person than a religious one, and I am fully aware that many of my beliefs do not jibe with traditional Catholicism. Nevertheless, my faith has given my life a foundation. By this I mean that I believe my life has purpose, no matter how difficult it can be at times.

Twice in my life I have gone to talk with a priest for guidance. And both times, each helped me tremendously. The first priest, Father Kenney, I met at a Catholic retreat when I was seventeen. I told him I was having doubts about my faith. I told him further that when I had confessed this to my parish priest, he responded by telling me that doubting my faith was a "mortal" sin. That, of course, did not help me at all, so I told Father Kenney I just was not going to Confession, or Communion, anymore. (Before Vatican II, it was a prerequisite for Catholics to go to Confession before receiving Holy Communion, certainly if there was a mortal sin involved.) Father Kenney, after hearing this, understood that there was no "real" priest for me. So, he told me that if I did not have a priest within twenty miles of my home, he could grant me a dispensation from Confession. I didn't drive at the time, so he granted me this dispensation so that I could receive Holy Communion without going to Confession first.

The second priest I talked with many years later, and I talked to him about my depression. He said, "Depression is your cross to bear." He told me this in a loving way, prefacing it with the fact that we **all** have crosses to bear. He also said to me, "We all have one life to live and one death to die."

Prayer means a great deal to me, and I pray almost every day. Most often, I pray to Mary or to the Virgin of Guadalupe, for these figures represent the feminine and mothers—and I am a mother. To my mind, mothers are (ideally) all merciful; mothers are all compassionate; mothers are all forgiving. Prayer makes me feel connected to something larger than myself. It helps me to worry less, and, in the words of an African American spiritual, "lay my burden[s] down."

I have read a great deal of spiritual literature in my lifetime, both Christian and non-Christian. I have read the works of Saint Francis of Assisi, Saint Teresa of Avila, Pema Chodron, Deepak Chopra, Saint John of the Cross, Meister Eckhart, Mohandas Gandhi, the Dalai Lama, Thomas Merton, Paul Tillich, the Sufi poet Rumi, and Jon Kabat-Zinn, among many others. Rumi's poetry resonates deeply with me, especially his poetry that talks about the "King," the "Beloved," and the "Bride and Bridegroom" as the union of the innermost parts of ourselves.

To my mind, God is not really a **he** or a **she**, but rather a kind of spirit, dwelling in all things. This is where my Catholicism, my reading, and my life experiences have led me. Depression has been a great negative force in my life, but it dwindles in comparison to my faith in God, to my belief that human beings can often transcend their suffering. Whether we live on after death is immaterial. My faith leads me to believe that Life, Nature, God, all are here, now, inside and outside of us, in this present moment.

When I go for a walk, when I go to church, when I pray (or sing praises), I live in the moment, concentrating on what I am doing right now. This philosophy of living, elucidated by both ancient and modern thinkers, is perhaps the most effective way for me to fight my depression. I am not sure I can be immersed in the now and be depressed at the same time.

Many ancient and modern thinkers have talked about living in the moment. One of these, Eknath Easwaran, a spiritual teacher who wrote many books and founded the Blue Mountain Center of Meditation in Tomales, California, was my therapist David's mentor when he was at UC Berkeley. (Easwaran taught there in the early 1970s.) Although I had heard of Easwaran before David mentioned him to me, I went on to read many of his books upon David's recommendation. Easwaran elaborates on the idea of living in the moment, which he calls "one-pointed attention," in his book *Passage Meditation.* The basic idea of one-pointed attention is simply to give full attention to whatever matter is at hand. For example, when we eat, we just eat and concentrate on eating, rather than eating and reading, or eating and talking, simultaneously.

One-pointed attention is a simple concept but one that is difficult to apply without self-training and discipline. For most of us, perhaps Americans, especially, we seem to think it is part of our manifest destiny to be constantly moving forward, to be constantly busy. And most of us have the misguided assumption that we should be, and surely are good at, multitasking.

When I have a major depressive episode, when my depression is above a 5 and the water is climbing, climbing—focusing on the ever-present moment is one very good thing I can do for myself. One-pointed attention is what I am working on day by day. But even more than this, in my most depressed moments when I am full of trouble "terrible" and despairing that my mood will never end, I must, like the young woman in the Carrie Underwood song, be willing to have the faith to just let go, and to let God, the most mysterious force in the universe, take the wheel.

10 ~ Thanksgiving

> I am grateful for what I am and have. My
> thanksgiving is perpetual . . . My breath is
> sweet to me. O how I laugh when I think of my
> vague, indefinite riches. No run on my bank
> can drain it . . . .
>
> —Henry David Thoreau,
> *Letters to Various Persons*

During a high tide, the sea deposits detritus, a wealth of it, on the seashore—bundles of seaweed, small and large pieces of driftwood, an array of seashells, dead and dying jellyfish—in infinite variety. These beach skeletons, as I call them, are often beautiful; they speak to the marvelous. After a high tide, I once found a tiny and delicate sand dollar, about the size of a penny, near a shale sea wall, perfect and whole. Granted, many things the sea leaves behind are broken, dead, or dying, but all become hosts or food for such things as kelp flies, beach hoppers, pill bugs, bloodworms, sand crabs, and bean clams—and these in turn become meals for birds. In nature, nothing is wasted; death becomes life. Every time I walk on a beach, I am reminded of one of my favorite lines by the naturalist Loren Eiseley: "life is multitudinous and emergent in the stream of time."[20]

High tides make tide pools possible, those rocky pools on the seashore where all kinds of marine creatures live—algae, sea slugs, octopods, and various kinds of Echinoderms, sea cucumbers, sea urchins, sea stars—in a profusion of vibrant colors. When my children were little, we spent much of one afternoon exploring tide pools in the Pacific Grove area of California. My son picked up a lavender starfish, and it stuck its tiny tentacles to my son's palm and little fingers, hanging on for dear life. I took a snapshot, and this remains my favorite picture of my son, where he is holding the starfish in his hand, gazing upon it with a look of pure amazement.

Although I can't say that my life has been an exactly happy one, if I had never suffered from depression, I am not sure who I would be today. Depression has both debilitated me at times and given me strength. It has made me a complex person, one who is compassionate, thoughtful, and deeper than I otherwise may have been. So, regardless of all of my troubles, I am thankful for all my suffering has given me.

When my therapist made that provocative statement about how other people would be jealous of what I had, buried beneath his words was the idea of gratitude. I understand gratitude. And I am grateful.

I am grateful for the light the morning sunlight brings and the darkness that covers the earth when evening falls. I am grateful—and amazed—to be living on this third rock from the sun, teeming with both life and beauty. For the streams, lakes, rivers, oceans, mountains, valleys, and for the flora and fauna that inhabit this remarkable planet with us, I am grateful. I am grateful for springtime, summer, fall, and winter, the great cycles of nature and of human life.

I am grateful for the universe, for all things visible and invisible, and for the great mystery that lies at the heart of all things. I am grateful for music, for those songs, classical, popular, and country, that resonate so deeply within me. I am grateful for books and authors, and those still to come, for great books inform much of who I am. I am grateful for that magic element found in so many stones on earth, which has given me a better life than the one I may have had.

Most of all, I am grateful for the people in my life—including my therapist, David, my friends, my sisters, my children and grandchildren, as well as for those who have passed. I am grateful that I was born and that I still have some life to live. I am grateful for my body, still working pretty well at almost sixty-four years "young," and for my mind, which, for all its suffering, remains both sound and whole. And, like Thoreau, I am grateful for all "my vague indefinite riches."

For all of this and more, I offer a prayer of thanksgiving.

Notes

1. William Wordsworth, "My heart leaps up when I behold," in *The Collected Poems of William Wordsworth* (Ware, Hertfordshire: Wordsworth Editions Limited, 1994), 91.

2. American Psychiatric Association, *Diagnostic and Statistical Manual of Mental Disorders*, 5th ed. (Arlington, VA: American Psychiatric Association, 2013), 124.

3. Kay Redfield Jamison, *Touched with Fire: Manic-Depressive Illness and the Artistic Temperament* (New York: Free Press Paperbacks, Simon & Shuster, 1994), 16.

4. William Styron, *Darkness Visible: A Memoir of Madness* (New York: Vintage, 1990), 44.

5. Kurt Vonnegut, *Mother Night* (New York: Dial Press Trade Paperbacks, 2009), v.

6. Sue Monk Kidd, *The Secret Life of Bees* (New York: Penguin, 2003), 28.

7. American Psychiatric Association, *Diagnostic and Statistical Manual of Mental Disorders*, 125.

8. Willem A. Nolen, "More Robust Evidence for the Efficacy of Lithium in the Long-Term Treatment of Bipolar Disorder: Should Lithium (Again) Be Recommended as the Single Preferred First-Line Treatment?" *International Journal of Bipolar Disorders* 3, no.1 (January 2015), doi: 10.1186/s40345-014-0017-6.

9. Jamison, *Touched with Fire*, 107.

10. Jamison, *Touched with Fire*, 105.

11. Robert M. A. Hirschfeld, Lydia Lewis, and Lana A. Vornick, "Perceptions and Impact of Bipolar Disorder: How Far Have We Really Come? Results of the National Depressive and Manic-Depressive Association 2000 Survey of Individuals with Bipolar Disorder," *Journal of Clinical Psychiatry* 64, no. 2 (February 2003): 161.

12. Leo Tolstoy, *Anna Karenina*, trans. Richard Pevear and Larissa Volokhonsky (New York: Penguin, 2000), 1.

13. Fernando Pessoa, *The Book of Disquiet,* trans. Richard Zenith (New York: Penguin, 2003), 211.

14. Joan Didion, quoted in "The White Album," *The White Album* (New York: Farrar, Straus & Giroux, 2009), 14.

15. Pessoa, *The Book of Disquiet*, 115.

16. "Virginia Woolf's Handwritten Suicide Note: A Painful and Poignant Farewell (1941)," in Letters, Literature, *Open Culture*, August 26, 2013, http://www.openculture.com/2013/08/virginia-woolfs-handwritten-suicide-note.html.

17. Jamison, *Touched with Fire*, 41.

18. Jamison, *Touched with Fire*, 42.

19. 7. 1. Matt. (King James Version).

20. Loren Eiseley, "The Snout," in *The Immense Journey* (New York: Vintage, 1957), 59.

Acknowledgements

I want to thank the following people who read various drafts of my manuscript and gave me support and encouragement: Jeremy Cropper, June Gillam, Phil Hutcheon, David Madden, Dennis McFadden, and Bob Rennicks.

I also want to thank the American Psychiatric Association as well as the editors at Simon & Shuster for allowing me to reprint copyrighted material.

Made in the USA
Middletown, DE
23 July 2016